AUDEN

An American Friendship

AUDEN

An American Friendship

Charles H. Miller

PARAGON HOUSE
New York

First paperback edition, 1989

Published in the United States by

Paragon House
90 Fifth Avenue
New York, NY 10011

Library of Congress Cataloging-in-Publication Data

Miller, Charles H. (Charles Henry)
    Auden : an American friendship / Charles H. Miller. — 1st pbk. ed.
       p.   cm.
    Reprint. Originally published: New York : Scribner, c1983.
    Includes index.
ISBN 1-55778-198-2
    1. Auden, W. H. (Wystan Hugh), 1907-1973—Friends and associates. 2. Miller, Charles H. (Charles Henry) 3. Poets, English—20th century—Biography. I. Title.
[PR6001.U4Z7595   1989]
811'.52—dc19
[B]   88-30124
                                                                                              CIP

Manufactured in the United States of America

To

> *Lynn and Lark,*
> *underwriters of my creative hours*

And to

> *Wystan Auden's readers,*
> *who may wish to share these memories*

AUDEN

An American Friendship

ONE

---

*A poet is a revolutionist
who wants to convert the reader
to his verbal society.*
"A Sense of One's Own Age," lecture, January 1940

W. H. AUDEN WAS TO MEET US UNDER THE FRONT ARCH OF THE
Union building of the University of Michigan in Ann Arbor at
noon on a January day in 1940. I was waiting with four other
student poets and four professors, one of whom was remarking,
"All I know about Auden is that he's an obscure Marxist poet
from Oxford who knelt before his King to receive the Gold
Medal for poetry!" I frowned at the snide professor, for Auden
was acknowledged to be the most committed poet of the times;
I regarded his recent book *On This Island* as a bible, and I
felt that our university was lucky to have Auden come to Ann
Arbor as a visiting lecturer.

Across University Avenue came a gangly young man, bare-
headed in cold sunlight, squinting toward us as he strode over
the half-frozen slush. He wore a sloppy brown tweed overcoat,
which was unbuttoned, revealing a tweed suit that looked as
if he'd slept in it (as he had, on the train). If Auden had
straightened up from his habitual slouch he would have appeared his nearly six feet in height, but he ambled toward us,
amiably or absent-mindedly self-confident, carrying a cardboard case of the type used by students for mailing their

[1]

laundry home to Mom. (When he casually opened the case later, we saw to our surprise only a few pencils, loose paper, a thin edition of Rilke in German, a carton of Lucky Strike cigarettes, and a blue-flowered silk Chinese "night gown" so gossamer it could be wadded into one hand.)

To us Auden seemed very English, with his pasty complexion, in contrast to our idea of ruddy Scotch, Irish, or Welsh. His face bones were noticeable, and his jaw seemed unlikely to sprout a beard; his brownish hair had streaks of tow or butter-yellow and was tousled, uncombed, unbrushed.

As Chairman Louis Bredvold of the English Department greeted him, I noticed that Auden had gulping lip and mouth movements. When he dutifully shook hands with each of us, the glances from his hazel-brown eyes seemed shy, his manner both curious and questioning, as if he was appraising each of us and might not defer to any of us.

At the round-table luncheon in the Union faculty dining room, Auden appeared at ease as he devoured institutional food with more appetite than etiquette, using his knife to load his fork, crushing flaky hard rolls to bits with his nicotined fingers. In one of the pauses I asked, "Mr. Auden, has soap opera infected radio broadcasting in England as it has here?" And his quick reply, accompanied by a nod and a slight smile was, "Uhm, ye-es, it has."

The luncheon closed with a relaxed half-hour of discussion in which Auden was also a willing listener as he slouched back in his chair under the cloudlet of his cigarette smoke, his easy manners inviting acceptance. Later that afternoon we went to the elegant Rackham Auditorium, where Auden delivered one of his first major American lectures, "A Sense of One's Own Age."

Auden had told Professor Roy Cowden of the English Department that he'd be pleased to meet student poets informally, so the next day a few of us went to John Brinnin's bookstore, the Book Room, across from Angell Hall, anticipating a bull session on modern poetry. But Auden casually made himself one of us, browsing the shelves and complimenting Brinnin on the wide selection of contemporary

English poetry, which was then dominating the American literary scene. I was surprised that Brinnin appeared shy and made no effort to talk with Auden, so I did, passing him a Dylan Thomas volume opened to "Hands have no tears to weep. . . ." Auden shrugged and drawled in bent-head baritone, "Hmmm, yes, I know that poem," and touched the page with his fingertips as he continued to browse along the shelves, turning to ask me politely, "Uh, what are you writing these days?" And I said, "Oh, I'm writing about the Dakota wheat fields, where I worked in the harvest last summer." Auden seemed interested in wheat fields as well as poetry while we talked by the front window, our backs to the snow-heaped campus.

"Mr. Auden, will you be here tomorrow? Yes? Will you come to our Poetry Club?" I asked eagerly.

"Hmmm, uh, how much do you pay for a reading?" he drawled, to my surprise.

"Oh, we don't have any money! I founded the club when I came here from Chicago last year. We read our poetry and talk about writing it, that's all."

So it was that Auden came to our penniless Poetry Club in a university seminar room, proving himself a more dynamic reader than lecturer, bending over his rumpled typescripts, intoning new poems in a forceful voice charged with controlled emotion. His accent was less of a problem for us within his metric lines, and he read as devoutly as if he were holding forth in an Oxford hall or standing before a joint session of Congress. It was an impressive occasion for our dozen or so apprentice poets, even for those of us who had published a few poems in national publications. We sat in attentive silence while Auden read "Law Like Love," "The Casino," and "As I Walked out One Evening." He also read his new poems on Freud and Yeats. Because other student poets had nothing to say, I ventured some remarks on artists' sensitivity, quoting Auden's own phrases from the Freud poem, and from the Yeats poem, "A few thousand will think of this day. . . ." But Auden firmly rebutted: "If one says, 'I am a lonely poet, I suffer more than John Jones of the Elks Club,' one has a false concept of suffering and sensitivity. We are all basically the same, we all suffer equally."

After the reading, Auden went his way into the winter dusk, but we found it impossible to return to our studies, despite final exams looming over us. Snow fell that weekend, followed by a dramatic drop in temperature. It seemed to me that the pure frosty air was a tribute to Auden, that the snow was heaped in his honor. Brinnin and I agreed that we couldn't let Auden escape without more socializing, so five of us pooled our pennies and dimes to buy a fifth of White Horse Scotch whiskey and headed toward Professor Cowden's house on Olivia Street.

As we scrambled out of the car, we could see Auden sitting near the window before a blazing hearth, talking earnestly with white-haired Cowden. As determined as commandos, we marched onto the ice-crackling porch, knocked, and told Cowden we wanted to talk with Auden. Cowden opened the door wide and bowed, to welcome us in; but no, we wanted Auden on our terms. He came out, squinting nearsightedly, and we thrust the handsomely wrapped bottle into his hands, Cowden standing genially aside. Auden commented, "Hmmm, thanks, but I *don't* like wrappings on books or bottles!" Saying which, he stripped off the wrapping, yanked the cork, and passed the bottle first to Ellen, our mascot-poet; then we all took a swig in turn, Auden drinking the last and most, capping the bottle with an emphatic "Aaah!" He stood hugging the bottle like a baby while he gently explained that he couldn't come with us, being a guest of the English Department. Cowden reappeared with shot glasses, but we declined to come in, shook hands, and abruptly hurried off across the snow.

Auden departed from Ann Arbor on Monday to continue a short lecture tour, leaving in his wake a local controversy which continued for some weeks. "A Sense of One's Own Age" had evoked some puzzled criticism. Well-publicized and well-attended, his lecture had attracted, as the Michigan *Daily* reported, "the largest audience of the academic year." Cowden's introduction had been brief: "There are two classes of poetry, ancient and modern. Of these, there are two types of poetry, good and bad. With great pleasure, the English Department presents W. H. Auden, who writes good modern poetry!" Auden opened his lecture with playful allusions to the auditorium's starry ceiling and the seductively cushioned seats, and began: "It is said that a lecturer is one who talks in others' sleep. . . ." After some random remarks about our life on the planet, with its "strong sense of community," Auden argued that "an inescapable sense of loneliness confronts the individual, because the Machine has destroyed community." Relationships were now a matter of choice, not of proximity. "The artist's duty is to recognize suffering, and to develop means of expressing his own suffering."

This wasn't what we'd expected of a lyric English poet, but Auden was actually explaining some of his past and much of his future poetry. The Michigan *Daily* reported that "Auden slowly, haltingly, at times almost incoherently, expounded" his themes of "our age" and "the community of man." Some in the audience walked out; and one local critic attacked the lecture as a "re-hash of a recent Auden essay in a New York periodical." But most students and all student poets were elated with Auden's unorthodox lecture.

By 1940, when I first met Wystan, I had kept a personal journal for more than ten years, so he fell naturally into my scribbled pages, where I jotted down these early Ann Arbor morsels:

> The machine has destroyed the neighbor, the person who is tied to us and whom we're dependent upon.

> Blake attacked Newton because Newton represented a world where reason was separated from emotion.

> Heroes of American novels learn and determine not to accept the way of life they find nearby.

I continued reading and rereading Auden's books, especially his new *Journey to a War* with its mixture of history, reporting, and politics, a profound commentary on the human condition, a commentary which outraced student minds. Following Auden's first lecture in Ann Arbor I went to Brinnin's Book Room and bought *Letters from Iceland* out of my very meager food allowance, but before I finished reading it, *Another Time* stood in the center of the Book Room display window. I bought it and reveled in the enduring poems he had read to us at the Poetry Club meeting, poems on Freud, Yeats, and Henry James, as well as those on Rimbaud, Lear, Melville, "The Musée des Beaux Arts," and the ambiguous love poem "Lay your sleeping head, my love, / Human on my faithless arm." Within a few months *The Double Man* would be published, proving that Auden was productive in America, and proving to us that student poets had to read swiftly to keep up with his outpouring of poetry.

In the following months I kept track of Auden via the poets' grapevine and read his new poems as they appeared in periodicals. The anthologist Louis Untermeyer came to the university for a month's residence, attending our Poetry Club and giving lectures, in some of which he derided Auden's poetry and impressed on us his own frivolity.

In late autumn 1940, the University of Michigan Press published *New Michigan Verse*, which included early poems by Roethke, Brinnin, Ciardi, and myself; during that winter I hitchhiked to New York City to visit a friend, with whom I attended an Auden poetry class at the New School and was pleased that Auden remembered me and called on me to recite. In May 1941, Auden judged the Hopwood Award poetry entries, giving my poems first place (although he couldn't associate my pseudonymous poems, "by Phillip Asbury," with my person). In June 1941, I graduated, cum laude.

With no advance notice, Auden returned to our campus in September 1941 to give a lecture course and to confer with student writers. He sent word for me to come to his office in Angell Hall, and there I found him, intent at his work desk, a cigarette in one hand, a manuscript before him. He was wearing baggy blue jeans, a drab brown polo shirt, and torn sneakers. His face lit up, he jumped to his feet and shook my hand.

"Charles! I saved a place for you in my course. But more important, you must share my house. Yes! Come, now! Let's go have a look at the house, and we can talk there." He was already seizing books, papers, his jacket, but I took a sideways step in the bare little office, shaking my head. "No, I can't, I'm sorry, but I'm renting a place with another grad student. I can't live with you."

Auden was intently lighting another cigarette off the butt of the old one, and eyeing me sternly as he stammered (a habit when he was nervous or excited), "A-aa-act-u-ally, now, you *must* live with me, because I'm a stranger here, and you're the only person I know in all Ann Arbor. You're a poet, Charles, and I'm told that you're an, uhm, accomplished cook. Let's go to the house. We can talk on the way."

I drove at Auden's directions to 1223 Pontiac Trail, a handsome new studio house which stood on the foundation of the house occupied by Robert Frost when he was the University's resident poet. Showing me through the compact dwelling, Auden proudly recited, "Now please notice the sensible design, the entry here, the kitchen just there, and here to the right is the living room, comfy despite its hugeness. See, the fireplace works perfectly—feel the heat it throws! Behind the fireplace is that work space, a balcony overhead where your guest, or mine, may stay on the couch. Come this way—my sleeping apartment is a half-flight up, yours a half-flight down, and the bath is on the landing between them. Look, Charles! Your very own room. Do you like it? You may have the most e-ex-tra-ordinary parties in there, and I shan't hear a thing!

"Come, let's look at the kitchen. Suppose we, uh, share household duties. I pay all expenses, except your liquor, but I provide the dinner wines. I'll wash up the dishes, clean rooms, that sort of thing. But since you're a cook, and a good one, I've heard, I shan't compete with you there. The kitchen's cozy, isn't it? Now! You go sit by the fire and I'll make tea for us. *That* much I can do."

I sank into a chair by the hearth, bemused, and Auden went to make tea. He returned in ten seconds, to put a record on the player: "Listen, now! Isn't it happy!" It was Offenbach's *Gaîté parisienne*, at full volume, nearly lifting the high ceiling higher, and I was already high enough, my thoughts winging about the house, uncertain as to whether I was captive or guest.

Auden soon strode into the room with the tea service on a big tray, and though I'd been braced for English tinned biscuits, he served commercial cupcakes. Handling the teacups abruptly, he poured tea and came to the point, just as the record ended.

"Now, Charles, you must know that I'm a homosexual!" he announced sternly, biting his lower lip, giving me a severe glance. "Hmmm, I dare say you don't know much about homosexuality, for most Americans don't. You may suppose you're not safe around me? Aa-aa-act-ual-lee, I've been in love with just one man for several years, and I don't want to go to bed with any other person. Here! Let me lend you this Freud volume on aberrations. Freud points out, correctly, that a homosexual may be normal in nearly every way, except the sexual. I-I-I, uh, am *not* interested in you sexually! And I am normal in most ways, as you've no doubt noticed."

I sat, deadpan, clutching my cup of tea, nodding gravely at his charged confession.

"Hmmm, do let me pour you some more tea, Charles. Don't you think it's good? My brother has a tin of it sent me, now and then, from India. I'm glad you like it, for I'm a tea drinker. Now . . . hmmm, yes, now—you may move in as soon as you please. Today, if you like. You *cahn't* refuse me, you know, for I have no other friend in this town!"

I sat there, trying to smile politely, trying to come down from the music, from the torrent of Auden's words, from the sudden idea of living in this house with this gangly but gracious man, so confident and so commanding. As a farm boy, I'd labored and hungered through the Depression, lived in basement and slum rooms, and had never enjoyed such a house as this. I was assaulted by the vision of a poet's happy home, visited by happy people ("your guest, or mine, may

[8]

stay . . ."), parties, teas, regular meals. And a room of my own, in which to write.

The house was austere, a bit lonely, far from the campus, and it was owned by Jean-Paul Slusser, an artist professor, who had tolerated no trace of cuteness in any corner, the rooms uncluttered and ready to serve the working muse.

Auden sat by the fire sipping his tea, chain-smoking, watching me, cat-and-mouse, as he nailed down his proposition: "Hmmm, now, *nye*-ther of us will be obliged to show up for a meal, hmmm, unless the meal is planned in advance. And *eye*-ther of us may leave for weekends or vacations—we mustn't violate our separate freedoms!" He leapt up to attend to the Offenbach record.

Relaxing before the fire I came to my decision, thinking, "All right, strange loneliness, I'll try to live with you!"

> . . . *Art and Life agree in this*
> *that each intends a synthesis.*
> "New Year Letter"

Next day I returned to Pontiac Trail with my antique Hupmobile sedan full of belongings collected from previous Ann Arbor nests. Auden greeted me warmly, opening the door wide to the September air, rationing small smiles and friendly phrases: "Good! So glad to see you. *Do* make yourself at home. And do let me help you with those things." So we lugged my boxes, bags and cartons, books and youthful treasures into my new room with its windows looking onto the garden. The bookshelves, work desk, and easy chair yearned for my presence, the small bed invited me: I had never had such a poet's room.

Auden took me on another tour of the house, "to master the gadgets," he said. With Professor Slusser's instruction sheet in one hand, he first confronted the thermostat on the living room wall, setting it for 65°F at day, 55° at night. Slusser's note warned, "Despite the usual guarantee, the kerosene water heater in the basement will not provide two baths the same morning or evening." Auden looked solemnly at me over the instruction sheet: "Charles, does this imply that two should bathe together?" I didn't think so, but managed a small chuckle to match Auden's contrived one. "Americans take too many baths, Charles! One or two a week should be enough, shouldn't it?" I emitted an Audenesque "Hmmm!"

We went to the kitchen to examine the electric stove and refrigerator (which Auden called a fridge), and he showed me the staple foods in the neat cupboards. "Here's the food list, and you must jot down the foods you want and those our meals require. I've listed coffee and orange juice, let's never be without them. And loaf sugar, which you call lump sugar, for our coffee and tea. Here's the petty cash in this tea tin. When you buy groceries, put the receipt in, and I'll, uh, put the money in, the same day."

Auden spoke proudly of the household he'd "managed" in Brooklyn Heights the previous year, but when he opened our broom closet he frowned at the dreary mops, brooms, garbage can (which he called a dust bin), and venerable carpet sweeper; there was no vacuum cleaner.

"There you are! You said you'd do the cleaning," I reminded him.

"Hmmm, did I? Aa-aa-act-ually, we might get a cleaning woman in, from time to time," he hedged, as we went out the kitchen door into the garden, which was dormant in cool September air, the grass unmown, the weathered picnic table set with delicate elm leaf doilies. Auden greeted the buckthorn and lilac shrubs in the easygoing garden, "It's almost English!"

As we stepped past the little garage, I said, "For your car, when you get one. My Hupmobile likes the outdoors," and Auden grunted in agreement. We glanced at the little cemetery above the side street, open fields and woods beyond it. An autumn breeze moved above the Huron River downslope, and Auden shivered in his cotton polo shirt, blue jeans, and unlaced sneakers. Wrapping his arms around his chest, he said, "I rather like this cool air. At least it's fresh. And did you know, Charles, that this is my first house with a garden and garage?"

He looked around the place proudly, youthfully, as we went in to have tea by the fire and talk about the days ahead. The large window flooded the living room with silvery gray light, and as Auden settled back in the blue-flowered wing chair he said, shyly, cautiously, "By the way, you must call me Wystan, that's my name! And you're usually called Charlie, aren't you?" And so we were at home.

Next morning I was up before seven and went into the living room to yank the cord that trolleyed heavy curtains over the big window, and *crash*, down came the curtain, trolley and all, onto the floor. Down came Auden to survey the wreckage and calmly set about to repair it. "Hmmm, first, let's remove the curtains. You work from that end. I think I know how this trolley works. Now, Charlie, fetch the ladder from the basement, please." His intense effort and my silent aid soon got the curtained trolley back on the track, where it obediently slid back and forth. "By the way, Charlie, you just might pull easily on the cord and let the curtain work in its own way," he said casually as I picked up the tools.

In a few minutes he was having his habitual coffee and orange juice at the kitchen table while I had my hearty farm breakfast, and now we were naturally "Wystan" and "Charlie." Breakfast was pleasant, our best meal of the day, always, with easy and uninhibited talk.

I spent that first morning in arranging my books and belongings, and containing my rampant emotions in the quiet house that ticked with Wystan's typewriter in the living room. As I started to prepare our one o'clock lunch, Wystan appeared in the kitchen doorway with a zippered handbag, announcing, "Hmmm, now, Charlie, I'm going to Chicago for a day or so. See you later." And he ambled down the street toward the station.

From my journal, Thursday, September 25, 1941:

> What pattern of events allows this young man from Midwest farmlands to be sitting in Slusser's studio house, sipping a drink, while my housemate, Wystan Auden, goes to Chicago for a day or so? I'm looking

at Slusser's paintings on the walls of this modern house, watching hearth flames, listening to trains huff and whistle down in the railroad yards, while smiling at the way in which our Wystan drafted me into this house.

Two days later I found Wystan at the kitchen table when I got up after seven, and he seemed glad to see me. "How was Chicago?" I asked, and he said sleepily, "Really, now, an easy trip. So convenient to walk down to the station and be in Chicago in four hours." He puffed cigarette smoke toward the ceiling and said tenderly, "I met my love there. We walked by the water."

Patiently, I waited to hear more about his love. At that time, Wystan's love was Chester Kallman, whom he had met a few weeks after his arrival in America. Wystan had given an Eastertime reading at the modest Keynote Club in Manhattan, along with Christopher Isherwood and Louis MacNeice, to benefit the Spanish Loyalist cause. Chester came to the reading and waited afterward to have a word with Wystan, telling him how much he appreciated Wystan's poetry. This had initiated their relationship.

It happened that I had met Chester in the late autumn of 1940 when I walked into the New School in Manhattan with a student friend; Chester and Wystan were coming down the stairway into the lobby, and I stepped forward to ask "Mr. Auden" if I might attend his New School class later in the day with my friend, one of his students. "Of course you may," he said judiciously; "just pay the fee, there in the office." He turned toward Chester, who was waiting one step behind him, then added in a friendly tone, "And how are things in Ann Arbor?"—to let me know that he remembered meeting me there, months earlier. Chester and I looked at each other with mutual curiosity. At that time Chester was a very fresh and youthful eighteen, blond and blue-eyed, well rounded in face and form. His expression was grave, even a bit anxious, compared to his later smiling self-confidence. Chester started down the stairs with Wystan, still looking at me openly, with curiosity, very boyish in woolen sweater and soft shirt, very much Wystan's nubile boy as they went their way together.

On Wystan's return from Chicago he asked me, "Do you enjoy being alone in a house for days on end? Yes? Hmmm, I don't!"

At breakfast we talked casually about Michigan, Wystan remarking on the faint bluish quality of the rural air, and we discussed Chicago, which was the scene of my recent past. Wystan spoke casually of Spain, China, Brussels, but never London. He loved talking but was also a devout listener, an alert questioner. Although I'd met and worked with many foreigners in my work-scrounging around the United States, Wystan was unique; he was no "type," perhaps because he was intense, charged, and eager to discover our open society. Although his voice instantly identified him as a foreigner in provincial Ann Arbor, his tones were clear and expressive. His English accent was unlike anything I'd heard, though it had the usual European querulous grace notes; and it was often mock-cranky, almost always ironic and challenging. I had to listen closely to catch his exact words and meaning, but this wasn't a burden, for Wystan's lively expression and his zest for life soon accustomed me to his odd accent and speech rhythms.

Wystan's conversation was laced with his questions and sprinkled with "really" or "really, now?" long before Americans used "really" in every other sentence. But Wystan's "really" sounded like "ray-ally" to me, and his "now" sounded like "na-ow," but they were uttered almost urgently, as a challenge to any listener from whom Wystan wanted to learn something new. His agreement was uttered in an emphatic, "raa-ther!" with the broad European *a* predominating in his first years in America; and he punctuated his speech with responsive "hmmm" sounds, or a "hmmm, ye-es," his "yes" sounding more like "ya-as," for he often drawled, and his *r*s were softly Southern or New Englandish, so that his frequent "dear" or "dear me" sounded like "deah." While he talked, he frowned, made faces, and seldom laughed, but gave one the impression he hoped to laugh; and as often as I could

I evoked a real belly laugh from him, to my own satisfaction.

Bit by casual bit, Wystan told me how he came to America. During his youth he had read and studied American literature—especially Whitman, Emerson, and Dickinson. He regarded the United States as (he said) "a free and open society" in which he could express himself freely. In the mid-thirties he decided that he, like many others, would become an American citizen if possible, and when he traveled and worked in Germany, Iceland, Spain, and the Orient, America became more and more attractive. His plan for living here was crystalized when he traveled by train from the West Coast to New York in 1938, after his stay in China. From train windows and during stopovers and short visits with European friends across the nation, Wystan got a good dose of America, the vast new land, the vigorous open society, the "democratic" energy he admired above the "clubby" kingdom in which he was born and raised. A few months later, Wystan was ready to move to America, and he sailed from England in mid-January 1939, arriving in New York with Christopher Isherwood.

They lived at first among immigrant friends, but Wystan soon found his own way and lived where he chose, as one more of that brilliant and disparate army of émigrés of the thirties, splendid stragglers from the Old World, a group that included Albert Einstein, Igor Stravinsky, Thomas Mann with his numerous tribe, Aldous Huxley, Niels Bohr, George Balanchine, Isaac Bashevis Singer, Vladimir Nabokov, and many more in various walks of life, a rich transfusion of Old World blood for our young nation.

Wystan told me that he immediately felt "free to create" in America, so that his work continued, unabated. Some fine poems were written in his first months in New York, and perhaps he was at the peak of his creative power when he came to teach in Ann Arbor in September 1941. He was to maintain very high standards, if not always at the peak, for more than three decades.

Our house at 1223 Pontiac Trail was cozy when autumn rains pelted the windows, and during our talkative breakfasts Wystan puffed his Lucky smoke at the weeping panes and declared, "Lovely weather! Just lovely for writers and scholars." I agreed while I continued to eat my big breakfast.

At first I felt some awe living in a house with Auden while he sat every morning in the living room behind a closed door, tapping out the first pages of *For the Being* on his European portable. But soon he became the familiar Wystan moving through the house under a sloppy halo of Lucky Strike smoke, coughing, mumbling his verses in progress. And I, his complete opposite, sat in my own room, where I struggled with my amateur fiction of Michigan farm life.

We were fairly equal in house habits, preferring cool rooms to blasts of heat, being capable of austere discipline at proper times. Regularity and relative peace were our staples, so it was soon obvious that I could retain my precious individuality even while I consciously served Wystan. I got to the kitchen a bit after seven, made a pot of coffee, and prepared orange juice (sometimes fresh, more often canned), these two liquids being his whole breakfast. He soon appeared with uncombed hair, a small smile, and a keen glance at me while he intoned a mock-gruff "Good mawning!" and slumped into his chair at the table.

Wystan often carried about the house a student copy book with black-and-white marbled cover and sometimes his thin Rilke in German, with blue-lined yellow paper protruding from it. With his pack of Luckies and his fingerprinted spectacles tossed onto the table, he would bend stoop-shouldered over his cup to break loaf sugar into his creamed coffee. Glancing at my plate of scrambled eggs and thick slices of hand-cut buttered whole wheat bread, at my glass of milk and perhaps a peach or banana, Wystan said one day, "Hmmm, wouldn't you like some porridge, as well?"

I looked at him: "Are you ribbing me?"

"Hmmm, not *at-tall!* You're a healthy vigorous man, you exercise a great deal, so you must eat a great deal."

One day at lunch Wystan frowned above a favorite dish, boiled cabbage, and asked, "Haven't we mustard to go with this cabbage?" I went and brought from the shelf a jar of commercial mustard, which he tasted suspiciously: "Why, this *nah-*

sty stuff is merely mustardy mayonnaise! Get some powdered mustard seed from the deli, mix it with olive oil, and that'll be *real* mustard sauce."

Next day we had "real" European mustard sauce.

When Wystan first told me that he preferred to sleep on an empty stomach and to write for five hours on a breakfast of coffee and orange juice, I put it down to his native crankiness, but he soon proved to me that his discipline served him well. "One must eat a good dinner at six, or six-thirty, never later than seven, for eating late induces dreams, sometimes disturbing dreams. As for breakfast, writing on a full stomach is like boxing or wrestling on a full stomach—impossible!"

So Wystan wolfed his lunch, for the simple reason that he'd had no substantial food for eighteen hours, and for five morning hours had expended as much energy as a farm worker. It was a pleasure to cook for such a hearty eater; Wystan sat down to his noon meal with elbows akimbo, loading his fork with his knife, and stoking his hungry belly. Sometimes we enjoyed a small glass of wine at lunch, but never beer. Dinners were more relaxed, with a bottle of Wystan's favorite California Pinot Noir and candles and music by the blazing hearth. Wystan was very much at ease and often recited, with a contented sigh, "No matter how *down* one feels, a good dinner always makes one feel better!" This was just a hint of the intense emotional life he led during his mornings of work.

Breakfast often included a lesson on English usage. If I said, "I'll go by the deli today," Wystan would quickly correct me: "Charlie, you mean that you'll *stop* at the deli." With such good "stops" I was on my way to better English.

At breakfast we usually planned the next day's lunch and dinner, Wystan gradually requesting his favorite foods. He asked for sweetbreads, to be sliced in thin strips and fried in olive oil; this proved to be a success. Soon he asked for calf's brains, which weren't easy to get. Our butcher suggested I go to the slaughterhouse near the railroad station; and there in a cavernous room in that decaying Victorian warehouse I found the foreman in his blood-smeared white smock. He politely sold me pounds of calf's brains—"still warm," he boasted. Broiled brains were a gastronomic occasion for Wystan, so I soon returned to the slaughterhouse, where workers in blood-stained coveralls would bawl out, "Here's the brain man again!" And, "Give the guy his daily brains!" And, "What would *he* do without *our* brains!" All of which I relayed to Wystan, to his great amusement.

One dinnertime I put a bulging loaf of potato bread on the board with our staple Liederkranz cheese, and Wystan frowned, pointing an accusing finger at a bluish tint on the loaf's edge. "W-w-what's this? Can't we just have our regular French bread?" I quickly answered, "Just try this bread!" He tried it, a smile dawning on his pale face. "Why, it's, uh, excellent!" And so the great regional potato bread joined our staple list.

One morning Wystan sat very quietly at the table, holding but not lighting his companionate cigarette as he said very softly, "I dreamed of my mother last night." His tone froze me. I sat waiting. "You know, Charlie, I lost my dear mother just a few weeks ago. I do, uh, miss her, very much." Amazed at this news, I waited until he added, more audibly, "We were very close. She was the dearest one in the world." He was close to tears, and I asked, as gently as I could, what caused her death. Wystan laconically recited some medical details as we soberly continued our breakfast. At last he picked up his pack of Luckies and said with his usual cheeriness, "See you later," and went into the living room where his portable typewriter was soon quietly clattering, with the poet in control as usual.

True democracy begins
With free confession of our sins.
"New Year Letter"

One morning after Wystan had heard me screaming in my sleep, he asked, "What did you dream? You must be deeply troubled, to scream out like that." He was tense with curiosity.

"My dream? Nothing much." I answered ironically, not intending to tell Wystan my troubles. But his sincere interest gradually overcame my restraint. "Well, I dreamt that I was running across a desert, like the Mojave. A man ran after me, shouting, waving a weapon of some kind, and I knew that he wanted to catch me, to kill me. So I dodged off the path into the sagebrush. But another man popped up out of the sand, intending to kill me. Then—aaah!—I saw that they were two of my older brothers!"

"Really! Your screams were terrible. How could your own brothers cause such terror in you?"

Slowly, haltingly, I began to tell Wystan my story: "I was the eighth of ten children, and my parents continually fought with each other. Not that we didn't have some wonderful times as a family, but, as I grew up, I noticed my mother often whispering and plotting with one or more of my older brothers against my father. The whispering haunted me. After a long quarrel, which went on for days, just before the Depression began, my mother threatened divorce if my father didn't sign over all the property to her. He did sign it over to her; and then an older brother of mine pressured my father to conduct the family business as my mother and brother ordained. Life was severe, not only on the farm but throughout the nation; and by 1935—when I was struggling alone in Chicago—one older and my only younger brother stayed on the farm with my parents, where quarreling and fighting continued. My father was then sixty-five, but robust and a compulsive worker.

"One day my two brothers argued with my father up in the vineyard, ordering him to leave the farm and work elsewhere, while they managed the place. He refused to agree to such a plan. They knocked him down, beat him, kicked him in the face, broke many of his teeth, and left him there while they went down to the house to take all the legal papers and valuables. They went with my mother to the county sheriff to file eviction papers against my father.

"My mother wrote to me in Chicago, 'I hope your father commits suicide, that would be best for all of us.' And my father did. He shot himself through the heart, alone in the barn at twilight . . . just six years ago this December. It makes for bad dreams."

Wystan was visibly shocked: "It's out of Dostoyevsky or a Greek tragedy! No wonder you have nightmares. Do you still see your mother? No? And how do you feel toward your brothers?"

"I'd enjoy killing the older one!"

We sat at table in the silent kitchen, town noises far away, and I felt unexpectedly relieved. Wystan puffed smoke at the ceiling and watched as I dried my eyes, finally declaring, "Charlie, I'll tell you what helps me with terrible dreams— just write them down in your journal or notebook. Keep paper and pencil by your bed, write the dream as soon as you awake. Use shorthand. Make one word stand for many: Desert. Running. Man like brother. Zigzag in sagebrush. Other men pop up. It's important to record the dream quickly, before it fades, before wakefulness intrudes. Once you write them down, the dreams will become more clear—that is, you will remember them more clearly, and that will help you to understand."

"Wystan! I do remember them. I can't forget them!"

"Hmmm. That's bad. But write them down as tersely as you can, and perhaps you will not have such bad ones."

Following his advice, I recorded my dreams in earnest. But then I began to have horrible war dreams, and one morning at breakfast I handed Wystan this transcription of a global nightmare:

I beheld the earth as I floated in space, impressed with its beauty, its botanic greens, earth browns, ocean blue-greens, until with horror I noted a great snake winding itself around the globe, twisting and turning a bit from side to side, rearing then falling back, thrusting itself forward to girdle the globe—for that was its intention. When it was half around the planet I saw with terror that another snake was headed toward it, at a right angle, at higher speed, bound to collide with it. Looking closely I saw that both global snakes were composed of human bodies in combat outfits, all loaded with weapons, all squirming with venom, with hatred, all writhing with murderous intent. The collision was close. My horror was boundless, for I knew it would be tragic. I awoke, shaking, sobbing, wet with sweat.

Wystan read the dream rapidly, nodding his head, murmuring some phrases to himself. "In color, too! Now, Charlie, do these war dreams recur?"

"Yes. With variations. My brothers often stalk me or set traps, or lurk overhead in order to fall onto me and finish me off. My brothers appear in the war dreams at times. Of course, my family's violence is related to war violence."

Wystan sat at the table, staring hypnotically at me. "Yes, Charlie. All violence is related. War is a horrible thing, but it's a reality we have to live with, for now. I can understand your pacifism, but I doubt that yours or anyone's will rid our world of violence and war. Gandhi's didn't. Yours won't."

I answered that I had no choice. Pacifism was my gut reaction to violence in human nature. We said no more about it for the moment, although it soon became an issue between us. I noted in my journal at this time:

I must tell Wystan that war, like sex, never solved any problem but its own—if indeed it can do that. War may subdue or pacify a people, or conquer and coerce, like sex, but it cannot show us how to behave, once we get out of bed or off the battlefield.

At one luncheon, I told Wystan that I'd once gone in desperation to a university psychiatrist recommended by my speech therapist (who was helping me to overcome stammering and speech block). "I was received by this distinguished elderly doctor, who started to outline my case history. He got my family horror story out of me in short order, though not in the way I told it to you. He interrupted me throughout the hour, telling me what I'd *have* to admit, and guaranteeing me that he could help me, if it took months, or years. I'd soon be a new man, he promised."

"How did your analysis go?"

"I never went back to him."

"Really! Why not?"

"Well, I couldn't accept his accountant's mind. He kept saying, 'Your type is inclined to do that kind of thing,' and 'You must approach this situation in a logical manner.' That tone! I refuse to be a type, as he defined it. I approach my situations in my own manner. He seemed to me to be a thought surgeon, and I didn't ask for surgery, just sympathetic understanding."

"Hmmm. Ye-es. But he might have proved to you that you share some guilt for your father's suicide, that you wished for your father's death, as sons do. . . ."

"Wystan! I didn't wish for my father's death. I was opposed to my brothers and mother all along. Of course my father was no saint, but he was more admirable in many ways than they were. I was on my father's side in those old family battles." I stopped, realizing that I was talking too much about "secrets" which might bore Wystan. But he was concluding with a maddening—to me—repetition of, "Really now, Charlie, all young men wish their father's death. Perhaps it's a good thing. It's only natural, you know."

I didn't know. And I walked out of the room, as I sometimes did in those days when I felt that I had nothing more to learn from the master's "lesson."

TWO

To set in order—that's the task
Both Eros and Apollo ask . . .
"New Year Letter"

"SIT DOWN TO YOUR WRITING EVERY MORNING FROM NINE TO twelve for thirty years and you're bound to accomplish something," advised Wystan, quoting his father-in-law, Thomas Mann. And Wystan did sit down to his writing every morning, from eight to one, with clocklike regularity, in the autumn of 1941. He liked the house, the neighborhood; and he had no hangups about his work time, about being interrupted by telephone, doorbell, mailman, or caller with legitimate business, but he would be brief with any such interruption.

"A cheery fire is so comfy when the weather is nasty," he declared, as we agreed to lay in a supply of firewood. I located local woodcutters, and one fine autumn morning when sunlight glanced off bronze-red leaves, two woodcutters arrived in an old truck loaded with seasoned logs; the four of us carried the wood into the basement by armfuls, the woodcutters winking and chuckling at Wystan's intense way of "hustling" (as they said) the wood.

Wystan was visibly pleased to have the wood neatly stacked in his basement, and he invited the men into the kitchen for a "cup or a nip." They sat themselves at the kitchen table, chuckling over their private jokes, while I put the coffee pot on the burner. "Coffee? Or tea? Or a drink?" Wystan demanded cheerily. A drink, they instantly decided, so I started for the jug of California wine, but Wystan scolded, "Now, Charlie, none of that *nah-sty* stuff!" and strode to the living room for our one bottle of rarely touched whiskey, the woodcutters twisting about with laughter, the older nudging the younger, both of them chorusing, "None of *thaat* nah-sty stuff!" Wystan seemed not to notice their amusement as he set out four jiggers.

The woodcutters were foresty creatures with lined, weatherbeaten faces and laughing blue-green eyes. They kept their red plaid hunting caps on and both wore patched red flannel shirts under bleached and patched blue overalls with leg cuffs thrust into felt and rubber boots. Both of them smelled of barn manure and mucky soil, and they couldn't have been more picturesque or more pleased as they leaned their elbows on our table, grinning as an attentive Wystan offered cigarettes. When Wystan stepped into the hallway to answer the phone, they were convulsed, repeating, "None of that nah-sty stuff, hah!"

Wystan sat on the high stool by the stove, questioning them about their little backroad farm, the amount of milk their cows produced, the "veges" they grew; "Now, can you make a decent living on such a small place?" Yes, they answered earnestly, yes, if only they sold enough cords of fuel wood, some fruit, and produce to "college folks." Wystan instantly ordered a bushel each of apples, potatoes, and turnips "for our larder," the "larder" bringing on another duet of chuckles and nudges.

As we sipped whiskey and talked about small farming, the woodcutters confessed they'd hardly traveled outside their county, so I mentioned that Wystan had circled the globe, observed wars, and written books. Wystan frowned and shivered his head warningly at my enthused tattling, then held his head high to take a dramatic drag on his Lucky cigarette in what seemed to me a parody of pride. But without voicing a provincial question, the woodcutting farmers smiled over their drinks, and soon the older man caressed and folded Wystan's check into an overall pocket. They clumped out the back door, and we went to our labor among books.

Wystan offered to autograph his books on my shelf, "And, uhm, correct some errors." He went into my room and started leafing through each of the books in turn, finding that I was an underliner and margin jotter. In the Notes section of "New Year Letter" he found I'd splashed a large exclamation mark beside his phrase "For the last time, psychology," and he chuckled, "Ya-as, there's just too much psychology," and he leafed onward, looking for spoor of my reading.

I stood watching Wystan as I recalled Sidney Cox attacking Auden poems while we students sat around him on a cloverfield by the Cummington School (where I held the poetry scholarship in 1938). At that time Cox sided with facile critics who scored Auden for being "willfully obscure," and Auden's poetry for "being of no lasting literary value." A budding Audenite, I had easily rebutted Cox.

After Wystan autographed his books and expressed satisfaction in finding such a collection in Ann Arbor, I told him that my favorite book was *On This Island*, which I'd carried with me when I followed the grain harvest in Nebraska and the Dakotas in the summer of 1939, the book traveling in my hobo handbag along with cotton socks, denim shirt, extra pants, and notebook. I'd practically memorized its pages, transposing such lines as "Far off like floating seeds" into Dakota wheat seeds, and finding his world poems an ideal antidote to lonely drudgery on hot, dusty harvest fields. I'd rested in many a dusky hay mow in a cloud of clover perfume on solitary evenings, reading lines he'd written in Christian-Marxist tension on other continents.

In America's epic Great Valley with its millions of acres of ripening grain I met no other Auden follower, nor did I meet any reader of poetry: I was a needle in a vast agrarian haystack. There were Auden followers on wheatland campuses, but I didn't set foot on any campus in that summer when I made a conscious quest for America's agri-soul. Not to mention a quest for cash to finance my next university year.

On Nielsen's wheat ranch near Sherman, South Dakota, Mr. Nielsen found me reading the thin blue Auden volume, and he grunted, "Ya like to read books, hah?" He pointed to a silvery silo top just visible on the flat wheatfield horizon: "That's the farm of Rölvaag's wife!" He rightly assumed that I knew Rölvaag; and later upon my lonely haystack I held *On This Island* before my eyes, a slim perspective rod measuring a golden-grained prairie sparsely peopled with ghosts of *Giants in the Earth*.

During the early autumn I bused Wystan about Ann Arbor in my antique 1930 Hupmobile with its six wire wheels (two of them mounted in front fender wells), and he admired that orphan "motor" from auto-glutted Detroit; but one morning my "new" 1938 Plymouth two-door waited beside the house, and Wystan frowned at it: "Hmmm, is *that* supposed to better the Hup?"

I flushed. "Well, the Hup had transmission trouble, and it's hard to get parts for an orphan auto. This car'll go farther faster, more economically, if not as picturesquely." But Wystan was staring past the Plymouth at falling golden leaves, and he said reverently, "Once I had a low Aston-Marton roadster which I drove on Oxford roads at insane speeds. One time I rolled it over in a damp meadow, but my friend, Robert Medley, and I escaped with but scratches and bruises."

Caroline Newton, one of Wystan's supportive friends in New York, sent him a check for $750 for a used auto, and we shopped around until we heard of a 1939 Pontiac coupe, green as a Michigan frog, offered by a couple leaving town. Soon Wystan was proudly driving his Pontiac around Ann Arbor, describing it as his "first motor in America," and joking with me: "My Pontiac motor on Pontiac Trail—lucky we don't live on Cadillac Street!" The Pontiac, which we ever called the green Pontiac, had a perfect engine, tight steering, and a "newfangled" gear shift mounted on the steering column. Neither of us suspected that this "first car" would be Wystan's only car in America.

Wystan said, "Come! Let's take a drive and get a bite to eat at that new Route 12 roadhouse." We started, and I noticed that Wystan's mastery of the Pontiac was impressionistic rather than mechanical, partly due to his shortsightedness. "Do you think this motor might do, hmmm, a hundred?" Wystan cried out, swooping through college town traffic toward the Detroit highway. I pointed out to him that the Pontiac speedometer dial registered only as high as ninety-five, wherewith Wystan floored the accelerator and we were soon doing ninety-five on the lethal three-lane Route 12, until he steered thrillingly to the left across two lanes to skid into the roadhouse parking lot in a glorious cloud of dust, testing and proving the brakes.

While Wystan wolfed his roadhouse snack, I ate gingerly as I tried to exorcise my belly butterflies from that moment when Wystan leaned over the steering wheel, squinted at the speedometer needle which was bumping the ultimate ninety-five, and yelled, "I bet we're doing over a hundred!" while I hallucinated local headlines: "English Prof and Student Creamed on Deathtrap 12!"

However, keeping my cool and my lunch, I sped onward with Wystan, who was to prove his luck at the wheel in wide-open America.

> *Have they ever, one wonders,*
> *Wanted so much to see a unicorn, even*
> *A dead one? Probably. But they won't say so.*
> "A Healthy Spot"

In early October 1941, in classroom 2215, Angell Hall, Wystan chalked onto the blackboard, "English 135, Instructor W. Auden," and turned to scan our faces, as if to memorize us.

"Now, no note-taking, please! You won't be quizzed on what *I* say, but on what *you* think about certain great books. Such as, hmmm, *The Divine Comedy, Augustine's Confessions*, four Shakespeare plays, *The Brothers Karamazov*— some twenty books, some you know already. I require that you read, in addition, certain American books central to our theme of fate and the individual in European literature. As well, I recommend that you study fifteen others. Then you must memorize six cantos of *The Divine Comedy*, as an exercise." He was interrupted by murmurs from the class, and a matronly graduate student protested, "Professor Auden! I've never memorized a page of *any* writing, so how could I memorize six pages of Dante?"

"My *deah* lady! Please, any adult can memorize a few cantos of metric verse. You know, some uneducated ham actors often memorize ten pages in one day. Hmmm." He stood looking innocently, mock-reprovingly, at the class, which squirmed before him on hard board chairs. As the murmuring continued, he nodded, conceding, "Very well, now, those of you who can't memorize six cantos shall be allowed to memorize, uh, four!" We sat on our oak seats, elbows and closed notebooks on the attached writing boards (so like big bread boards), and our instructor talked intensely if amiably while he passed out mimeographed outlines and required reading lists.

In addition to Shakespeare and Dante, this list included *Moby Dick*, *Agamemnon*, Horace's *Odes*, Pascal's *Pensées*, Jonson's *Volpone*, Racine's *Phèdre*, Blake's *Marriage of Heaven and Hell*, Kierkegaard's *Fear and Trembling*, Ibsen's *Peer Gynt*, Rimbaud's *Season in Hell*, Kafka's *The Castle*, T. S. Eliot's *Family Reunion*; and eight opera libretti, including *Tristan and Isolde*, *Don Giovanni*, and *The Magic Flute*.

A list of recommended reading included Benedict, *Patterns of Culture*; Mead, *From the South Seas*; Lynd, *Middleton*; Chadwick, *The Heroic Age*; L. P. Ker, *Epic and Romance*; R.M.S. Crossman, *Plato Today*; C. N. Cochrane, *Christianity and Classical Culture*; C. S. Lewis, *The Allegory of Love*; P. Wickstead, *Dante and Aquinas*; Wyndham Lewis, *The Lion and the Fox*; T. S. Eliot, *Selected Essays*; Nietzsche, *The Case of Wagner*; Thomas Mann, *Past Masters*; Empson, *English Pastoral*; Valéry, *Variété, I, II, IV*; H. James, *The Art of the Novel*; Denis de Rougemont, *Love in the Western World*; and D. H. Lawrence, *Studies in Classical Literature*.

It was no snap course. Yet, we had read some of the books, and now most of us were eager to read the rest, to get with those great books, to digest fate and the individual. Our instructor established a stern radical tone, and every serious student was ready to accept the discipline. Most of us had good reasons for electing the course: several of us were published writers, some were taking honors courses, and more than half of us were graduate students. There was one English Department instructor as well as two departmental graduate assistants, so that the class was more truly a seminar than a course.

Auden stood before us in jersey shirt, blue jeans, and torn sneakers that were usually unlaced. Often he paced from the window wall to the hall door as he talked intensely, not lectured, to us, his pile of books and papers untouched on the desk behind him, his remarks cruising the cosmos in an impassioned monologue, with Pascal's *Pensées* a leitmotif in early autumn sessions. In effect, he recited his thoughts on the great books, pondering aloud their import and implications. He stressed the books' ideas and rarely if ever mentioned their style; he pursued authors' hearts and brains, not their personalities or appearance. But he didn't stick to that little list; he rambled universally, globally. I scribbled in my pocket notebook: "Contain *what*?—first, contain the cosmos."

Although there were several "refugee" teachers and foreign students on campus, Wystan was an exotic "first" to most students, some of whom weren't inclined to admire his informal, if not sloppy, appearance, his Yorkshire-Oxfordized accent, and his highly individual mannerisms. Early in the course he pronounced "ate" as "et," and when a student timorously questioned the pronunciation, he defended it as "perfectly correct Oxford usage." At home, I assured him that only unschooled rural Americans or immigrants said "et," no matter how Oxford it was, and that its use startled us. Nodding his head silently, rapidly, Wystan accepted my advice, and I never heard him say "et" again, though he may have said it outside my hearing.

Our instructor cherished all the writers on the reading list but mentioned Melville often, assuring us that Melville "was

European in his awareness of evil." When he got to Shakespeare, he drew blackboard diagrams to show that Othello was stupid and that Iago was the most honest character in the play. I wasn't the only student to be put off, or let down, by his seeming flippancy toward Shakespeare; few of us had known so unorthodox a teacher, and none of us had known such a *presence* with such methods. When students discussed our instructor with me, I compared him to Sidney Cox, "a great teacher of mine at the Cummington School," an informal tutorial mentor. My journal notes:

> Often in class Wystan seems to employ obscurity, as if to conceal exactly what he means, what he intends. And sometimes he seems incapable of coordinating various ideas, so that some students say that he lacks sympathetic understanding for them. But I say that he's a radical poet lecturing to us.

Despite, and not because of, his eccentricities, our Oxfordian in Ann Arbor gave us an irreverent but revealing approach to selected classics. A few students were annoyed by his puckish remarks on Shakespeare and Melville, just as some of his prophetic remarks had offended some faculty and some reporters at his lecture, twenty months before, in Rackham Auditorium. One conservative student poet dropped the course, alleging, "Auden is evil and cynical about the classics," a view not shared by all of us.

Some student and faculty criticism must have originated in jealousy and some in lack of comprehension of Auden's puckish intellect, in which *play* with ideas as well as with words was ever-present. Looking back, we know that thousands of students, scholars, and professors have come and gone since Auden gave his English 135 course in 1941–42, a course which amounted to an individual monument at the University of Michigan.

Closing our first class session, Wystan announced, "It is my custom to have an at-home for students, where we may be as informal and sociable as we please. The address is 1223 Pontiac Trail, the time is after dinner on Friday evening, and all are welcome. Thank you."

The first at-home proved such a social success that the dean of women phoned the house next day and demanded some facts from me, which I calmly supplied: Yes, there was a liquor sideboard in the house, but no one was coaxed to drink. The dean told me, in campus-ese, that a student had returned to her residence hall "so intoxicated that she offered to fly from a fourth-floor balcony!" I was very, very sorry about this, and, as the dean requested, I got "Professor Auden" on the phone. He was even sorrier, but he assured the distaff dean that he'd regarded all the students as "adults. I *do* say that they were *quite* well behaved, so that I had no *idea* they had par-taken too much, for they left quietly, in good order." Standing near Wystan by the phone, I could hear the dean's official orders crackle forth: "No more liquor on the sideboard, and if a recurrence . . ."

Wystan and I sat sighing and chuckling at the kitchen table. "Really, now, Charlie, why *did* they drink so much? After this they shall bring their own beer, and we'll provide, uhmmm, coffee! Right?"

Even though this first at-home was big and boisterous, Wystan tried to talk with each of his students, to make our at-home more vital than a fraternity or sorority mixer; and it was livelier and warmer than similar receptions at, say, Professor Cowden's, but even so Wystan had hoped for more charm and coziness. Home meant much to Wystan, for his class and office hours amounted to five hours each Thursday, with campus politics, university affairs, and the English Department nicely separated from his daily concern with his own writing.

Isolated and protected as we were, there remained one invisible, infectious presence that poisoned all conscientious minds: the war in Europe and China, which proliferated daily toward a predicted world war. Our every action, thought, hope, and dream were colored by the consciousness of war, all the colors of dread, with shades of fear and anger.

Yet, Ann Arbor life could be petty, as when campus characters greeted me: "Charlie! You're still over there on Pontiac Trail? You know, you're getting an awful reputation, living with Auden!" I answered as bluntly: "You worry about your reputation, I'll worry about mine." At the same time, certain provincial professors worried an old campus bone: "How *did* Auden get a teaching contract here?" I happened to know how Auden got to Michigan, and the archives support some of my knowledge.

Perhaps it started even before we welcomed Auden in January 1940, toasting him on Cowden's frigid porch, warming the idea of a poet in the English Department; for Angelyn Stevens, John Brinnin, and I had praised Auden's poetry to English Department professors. Even so, the department was wise in securing Auden as resident poet, if disguised as an instructor. What we had originally expected of our English Department was *poetry*, and we promoted poetry in our Poetry Club, in Unitarian church readings, and in off-campus classes given by graduate students. Poetry was one of my expectations when I came to the university from Depression Chicago in 1938, alert with bodily and spiritual hunger, lean and pure as a wheat stalk, a frosty poet of twenty-five years, a late bloomer. As an active undergraduate, I had promoted poetry and attacked an English Department professor who had sneered at Auden's poetry; months before Wystan Auden came to teach on campus, I had written the following:

> To the Editor:
> . . . W. H. Auden, and many of the young writers you advertise as being too rotten to listen to, are just the ones I'm listening to: they are the true spokesmen of the large and terrifying real world beyond the . . . campus.
> (Michigan *Daily*, May 2, 1941)

This letter was answered by an elderly and venerable professor, who questioned my right to attack any professor in the "official" Michigan *Daily* newspaper, and I obliquely answered his letter by widening my attack to include the entire English Department:

> . . . The squabble about W. H. Auden's poetry is not a separate incident, but is closely allied to the fate of modern poetry in this university. . . . Looking back into old [university] catalogues, I find that courses in Modern Verse were listed each year and each year listed "omitted," and, "omitted 1940–41.". . . Other colleges offer modern verse, not only in their catalogues but in their lecture halls. The student body shows its willingness to elect such courses . . . will the English Department see fit to give them?
>
> (Michigan Daily, May 6, 1941)

The department didn't offer the course in modern verse, but it soon offered W. H. Auden, who appeared on the campus in September 1941, only weeks after the exchange of letters in the *Daily*; but his one course was not listed in the catalog. Whether Wystan had ever seen the letters, I didn't know, but one day he came home from the campus and said, very gently, "I, uhm, just now heard of your defense of me in the *Daily* last May. Uhm, good for you!" I mumbled, "It had to be done," and we never spoke of it again.

Thus, despite and because of controversy, Wystan came to Ann Arbor, and he had good reasons for choosing the University of Michigan. He wanted "to find America," and Ann Arbor was a likely place to find it.

One morning Wystan flicked his breakfast Lucky at invisible ghosts and began an amiable tirade, which I transposed in shorthand into my journal:

> Charlie, it's *amazing* that no one has really written about the true America, the land of the lonely! The land of eccentrics and outcast lonelies. "The Lonelies" could be the title of a grand unwritten American novel. I've been told of a likely hero, the homosexual "queen" of Niles, Michigan, you know? Each evening when the New York–Chicago train pauses there to put off a passenger or so, this lonely queen meets

the train, hoping to encounter one of his own kind. By profession, he's an accountant, but actually he's a loner who solicits traveling salesmen. His stand-by source of sex is high school football players who are coached not to "do anything with women."

Wystan chuckled and took a sip of his cooling coffee, giving me a quick little glance now and then as he continued talking avidly: "Imagine it, Charlie. Imagine such a scene being repeated daily in hundreds of dismal little American towns! Imagine all the small-town queens who have a flat or a cottage graced with their few books and records, perhaps some choice pornographic photos. Such queens may speak with an affected accent or lisp, trying for individuality; they idolize New York or Hollywood, but never escape the hinterlands." Wystan sighed heavily. "America *is* one of the loneliest places on this planet. And my friend George Davis ought to write a novel about it, titled 'The Lonelies.' "

"Hasn't Sherwood Anderson written it already?"

"Perhaps, in his own way. But the novel needs to be written by one of us." Puffing intently on his cigarette, Wystan continued, "There is always hope for a 'lonely,' always a chance that the lonely may find someone. For actually, any place you go, any place *on earth*, may have someone, if only you can find that one!" He finished, staring into the gray cloud of smoke he puffed toward the window and the lonely world beyond it.

Determinedly eating my breakfast so that I could go to work on my own kind of Michigan novel, I thought of the "lonelies" I'd glimpsed in little towns in four dozen states of Depression wanderings. In jerkwater stations where horizon-racing ribbons of steel rails were saddled with oily black platform planks, where the locomotive grudged to a halt, its oily pistons poised like lean legs trembling to pump across the prairie, where knee-high clouds of steam rolled along the platform to caress democratically all classes of travelers, there I'd seen the station "lonelies," their faces resolute as those of religious martyrs, their eyes shining with deprived love.

In 1941 I couldn't believe that Wystan was one of the "lonelies," but in time he would prove to me that he was.

Wystan overflowed with philosophy, advice, and precepts, some of which I jotted into journals and notebooks. (In truth, Wystan poured out cascades of words, of which I caught only cupfuls.) I especially cherished his precepts:

Three hours alone each day. (Easily done, here!) Eight hours regular sleep, preferably from 11 P.M. to 7 A.M., especially important for writers. Sleep on a fairly empty stomach, or risk bad dreams. Write on an empty stomach, with a clear head.

Any society which numbers individuals upon a blueprint is despotically dangerous, for it's too easy to erase the numbers.

The person you really need will arrive at the proper moment to save you.

Love and marriage are the most demanding of human challenges, and their long-term responsibilities make child's play of the average affair or attachment.

If one can't keep faith, one is lost.

Whatever a lover may do to or with his loved one is all right, as long as he considers the well-being of his beloved.

If you desire to make love to many different women, you'll find that it can be done. You may be amazed at the way you can acquire an effective seductive technique, but the more women you make love to, the less you'll be likely to find love, the real love, that has a religious basis.

This was a good dose for one day, but in my journal I pondered one important point:

I can't believe with Wystan that the person you really need will be given you at the moment of your greatest

[34]

need. Perhaps at times a person will be given, but not
every time.

I was thinking, here, of my father's suicide, of the many persons who perished for lack of love.

After our first clamorous at-home there was a later one
when students filled the rooms with smoke, excited talk, and
record music. When the talk centered on literature, Wystan
was in his bull-session glory, glad to hold forth on any subject.
He gave an eloquent appreciation of *Moby Dick* and then of
"Billy Budd," emphasizing Melville's "consciousness of evil."
One of the ₎udents interpolated remarks on his adored Hemingway, wiḷh the result that Wystan proceeded to dissect and
dismember that current cultural hero, although he did choose
to praise some of Hemingway's early stories set in Upper
Michigan. Annoyed, a *Daily* journalist said to me, while glar-
ing at Wystan, "Look at Auden, sitting there like he's on a
throne. Let's get him!"

Wystan, swinging one leg over the padded arm of the pale
blue wing chair, must have heard the student's battle hiss, for
he faced him with shining eyes, his head cocked in readiness,
his faithful Lucky glowing in one hand, to be waved like a
scepter as he went on: "Hemingway is not a political novelist,
as you claim. Not a-tall! He's an ambitious writer, a good
journalist but ingenuous in politics, though I dare say that he,
uhm, learned a bit in Spain, recently. That novel, *For Whom
the Bell Tolls*, is as romantic as his others. But not as good as
the others. Especially not as good as, uh, *Farewell to Arms*,
which you might do well to reread. A-a-act-ually, now, Hemingway is a fairly good journalist who seeks fame and lots of
money for writing popular novels," Wystan finished calmly,
with no malice, but the student journalist was enraged. He
excitedly proclaimed that "Hem" was "the greatest," and tried
to prove that Hemingway was "the Tolstoy of our day."

Wystan shook his head: "No, no! You'll find as you grow
up that Hemingway is not a whole novelist, that he lacks soul,
that he can't represent a whole society or a whole world, as the

great novelists are required to do. Parts of our world he does represent. And he has good prose technique, of a certain kind. Now, what do you think of E. M. Forster, or Isherwood's *Berlin Stories?*"

The students didn't know Forster, they had just heard of Isherwood; and the student journalist who couldn't "get" Wystan went to get some more beer. As armies of empties formed on coffee tables and in the kitchen, Wystan frowned and said aside to me, "Michigan students certainly aren't over-informed on modern literature!"

The evening tailed out on football; American versus imported beer; a bit on the coming war; and quite a bit on that old whipping boy, the English Department. Wystan remarked, "Imagine it! Two hundred-some teachers in the English Department. It's like the mass production factories in Detroit." Despite the wide range of talk, I felt that few students appreciated Wystan for what he was, a world poet with wide experience in literature and education; but we were grateful that the party was civilly pleasant.

At lunch one day Wystan asked, "Charlie, may *we* lend your copies of *my* books to a friend for a few days?"

As I hesitated, Wystan flushed, jabbing his cigarette into the ashtray as he mumbled, anxiously "I, uh, don't happen to have copies with me. Uh, will you?"

"Well, it's asking a great deal," I groused, "but *if* the books are returned, and I mean soon . . ."

Wystan jumped up and headed for my room, I at his heels. "I promise they'll be returned soon!" he vowed. I watched him pull half a dozen of his books from my shelves and dump them onto my desk. Opening the *Poems*, 1934 edition, he turned to the inflammatory, "Brothers, who when the sirens roar / From office, shop and factory pour," and marked the poem out, stroking his fountain pen strongly from the upper left to lower right of each page, leaving great black ink splotches.

"But Wystan! I like that poem . . ."

"But I don't like it, and I wish it weren't in this book!"

he retorted, his face reddening. He went through the books, correcting typos and excising poems while I growled, "You're renouncing!"

"Yes! One must renounce when one learns how wrong one can be!" And saying this, he calmed down. He turned to "Spain," marking out much of the long poem, and went on to other poems, recanting, revising. Aspects of the Auden I'd admired for years were dying before my eyes; in my political naiveté it hadn't occurred to me that I might ever renounce anything I passionately believed, and here was my poetic-political mentor busily renouncing his recent beliefs.

For a day or so after this ink-blotting and mind-slashing scene the house seemed as unreal to me as my recanting teacher; but our talks continued, Wystan gradually reemerged as Wystan the poet, and the rooms were reenlivened under our cozy roof on a quiet street over the river and across the tracks at the edge of a university town as yet untouched by the terrors of war in that autumn of 1941.

THREE

*All Mathematics would suggest
A steady straight line as the best,
But left and right alternately
Is consonant with History.*
"The Maze"

ON ONE OF THOSE CRISP AUTUMN MORNINGS WE HEARD BIRDLIKE cries of schoolchildren romping up Pontiac Trail on a chaperoned field trip to the countryside. As Wystan squinted through the kitchen window at those prancing young bodies in their bright coats and gaudy socks, I was nostalgically reminded of my crossroads school near Jackson; but Wystan was musing, "Hmmm, boys and girls, together."

Slumping back into his chair, lighting another cigarette, frowning through stringy blue smoke at the past, Wystan went on: "You know, Charlie, I'm the youngest of three brothers, and I can't remember being alone with a girl in my early years. At times, I had a nanny at home, an older woman, but we were all sent to boarding school, where an older boy or a man might take charge of a young child. And when a master whipped or punished a child, there was the older boy, or a dormitory proctor, waiting to take him in bed to comfort him. Really, it was quite natural to become queer, like them." Wystan rambled on, enlivened as usual in confiding to a friend, without a trace of rancor in his voice.

"But Wystan, didn't the proctors and masters try to restrict the boys to their own beds?"

"*Deah* me—quite the contrary. Proctors and masters had their pick of the boys. And if they were married, no matter; they still might be attracted to a boy. That's the way it was," and he smiled slightly at the rosy tip of his cigarette.

Like most "squares," I was curious as to how a male became "queer." I asked Wystan if the process were psychological.

"Deah me, of course it is. I just described it. In my case, it began with a need for comforting and understanding in a boarding school, the perfect forcing bed for the growth of the psychological homosexual."

Wystan spoke several times about corporal punishment in his boarding schools and the little world of boys' beds in dark, parentless dorms; but he never blamed his own parents, nor did he discuss his brothers. Several times he opined that mothers had a great deal to do with their sons' homosexuality, but he rarely discussed his father, much less conjectured on any father's role in his daughter's homosexuality. As for my own powerful mother, whom we discussed at various times, Wystan called her Clytemnestra, or my Grecian mother, but didn't try to equate her "power" with my own normal sexuality.

"My own queerness is an act of God—not that I'm against God, nor is he against me," Wystan proclaimed more than once, leaving me shaking my head. "Let's see, now: he's queer because of boys' boarding schools, but that's an act of God . . . then there's his mother—oh, my God!—I mean, his God. Well, it must be some form of blessing to be fairly normal!"

Although Wystan spoke to me of his early home life, of family ritual, books, music, hymns, rambles, good food, prayer, and games, he never got sentimental. He made slight mention of his brother John (none of Bernard), but he spoke of his mother as "the pillar" of his youth, and he didn't have to point out that he never leaned on her after his youth. In our first days together he seemed firmly in control of his emotions, but it was soon obvious that he was suffering from loneliness, sexual loneliness. Turning from his early theoretical comments on manners in America, he began to make specific and clumsy allusions to sex:

"Chester told me how a fellow sat in the bathroom

methodically masturbating until he saw himself in the mirror, and he slowly tapered off his stroke: 'It's no use—I'm just not *my* type!' "

Along with Wystan, I laughed as dutifully as I could, after hearing this joyless joke for the nth time in factories, box cars, hotel kitchens, college dorms, and locker rooms. Yet the joke's sad, psychological humor ensures its indefinite survival.

When we went to the then popular Flautz Tavern for beer and very good plain food, Wystan said, "This place is all right, but isn't there a *common* place where the, uh, workers go? A kind of beer hall?"

Yes, there was such a place, on Ashley Street near farm supply dealers, a big bare "cafe," and there we went on a gray autumn afternoon to sit among empty tables until a waitress approached, eyeing us warily. When I asked, "Have you any Canadian ale?" Wystan broke in, "Now, Charlie, none of that! We'll have just what the others are having! Two beers, please." The waitress's eyes had surveyed Wystan's unkempt Harris tweed jacket and unsoiled blue jeans, as well as my blazer with sport shirt, so she pinned onto us that invisible and damning label used by the Ann Arbor townspeople: "College crowd." We sat before our mediocre beer and talked desultorily about the world beyond the cafe.

Wystan was questing for his "common America," but I doubted that he'd find it on Ashley Street. Even my own authentic "commonality" was eroding in Ann Arbor. True, I'd roomed in a converted coal bin in a Chicago basement and stood in a few bread lines; I'd walked the asphalt miles more than once from the Near North Side to such places as Oak Park and back, for lack of car fare, in desperate search of subsistence work. I'd entered my share of seasonal box cars and hobo jungles while following various grain harvests in the thirties, but now I was a traitor to my lowest class—a collegian! That is, what aspiring farm boys thought a collegian to be: I'd earned prizes, awards, and a cum laude degree, as well as publication, and I was a bit of a snob. I dreaded hunger, privation, and the humiliation of poverty because I'd experienced it. In Chicago in 1935 I'd earned $185. I was lucky to earn that much, and I'd been able to subsist on it, while millions of healthy, trained, skilled, and talented workers earned less. Millions earned nothing. And here I was a Depression graduate, in the university of my choice, receiving Hopwood Awards and living in a comfortable studio house with an accomplished world poet. Of course I cherished my new status. And if Wystan quested for his "commonality" (allied in my mind with familiar Depression poverty) he was welcome to it. I willed it to him in discreet words while we sat self-consciously in this sad cafe.

Wystan never mentioned the cafe again so I never knew whether or not he circled back to it during his Ann Arbor quest for "common America," but I did feel that he would find no persons more representative than the milkman, mailman, mechanic, and woodcutters whose quotidian trails we crossed.

Wystan stood near the big window by his work table reading the Michigan *Daily*: "Charlie! Do you like the Quiz Kids?" He read aloud: "'Quipping Quintet to Face Faculty Five!' You know, Charlie, those little monsters devour encyclopedias and dictionaries. They can answer among themselves almost any question, and they're great fun."

With little advance notice, Wystan was named one of the "Faculty Five," and on the appointed night he took his place on Hill Auditorium platform while I sat down front. Hill Auditorium was the Carnegie Hall of the Michigan hinterland, imposing and hallowed with ghosts of international performers in passage; and on this night it held a fair crowd of several hundred Ann Arborites who wanted to observe the Quiz Kids in action.

They sat up there in cap and gown on one side of the stage, the professors on the other. Gerard Darrow, aged nine, solemnly peered from under his mortarboard and elicited audience response when he tried to recite whole pages of information he'd memorized concerning water lilies or diamond mining in Africa. Most of the professors were defensive and visibly unamused at the brain battle, but Wystan was in his unabridged element, mumbling answers under his breath. A Kid soon trapped him by reciting lines Wystan had written and published on education in 1932 and subsequently forgotten. But Wystan could still say, "Great fun!" and join in the applause when the vote tally was announced: 440 for Quiz Kids, 390 for Faculty Five.

Having joined the Ann Arbor Cooperative Society, Wystan wanted to observe a university student cooperative house, so I arranged for us to be invited to Karl Marx House near the campus; we drove there on a rainy evening and entered through a dark porch that shut out any possible sunlight from the front room. The Phi Bete student who had invited us wasn't there to greet us, so Wystan and I sat alone, looking over the dog-eared Marxist and party-line books in orange-crate bookshelves until dinner was announced in stevedore tones.

We squeezed in among the untalkative house members on rickety wooden benches, and faced a meal of mushy boiled potatoes, watery stew, stale bread, weary tea; for dessert, an emphatically day-old damaged Danish pastry. The food reflected the $2 per week for board and room, but the members ate heartily, noisily, and without conversation, despite my lively efforts to initiate some fun above the audible march of molars over food.

As the meal munched to a speedy end, my co-op friend said gently, "Brothers, we have distinguished guests with us . . ." But the house chairman, rising to his feet and wiping his mouth with the back of his hand, said sternly, "Skip the distinguished shit! We can see that we have visitors, so let's get on to house business. First, Brother Bernstein is a week behind in payment—pay up before noon tomorrow, Brother! Next, who'll volunteer to pick up the day-olds at the bakery tomorrow afternoon?"

I sat behind my best co-op house smirk, in sympathy with house routine, while Wystan lit up a Lucky and passed his pack around the table, unsurprised that it returned empty but for one cigarette. I was aware that the chairman suspected us of slumming at Karl Marx House, and so we were, in a way; but we were soon free to leave, and we did.

Driving homeward, Wystan complained, "Such poverty of spirit! How can they afford it? True, they're poor, many students are, but they're not required to be poor in spirit, and they just might be civil to visitors if not to each other. And that doss-house fare!"

As we sat before our flaming hearth, I thought of Wystan's "camps" in Iceland, Spain, and China and compared them to Karl Marx House. Could this be his worst?

"Wystan! There are nicer co-op houses, with clever students and decent dinners. Like my old Rochdale House."

"No thanks," Wystan said cheerfully, smearing Liederkranz cheese on potato bread. "I've had my fill of co-op houses for now." And he uncorked a bottle of Pinot Noir.

I sat staring at the generous oak and maple flames in the fireplace, thinking of the smell of Karl Marx House, the sounds of penurious life, the sharp voices of the house members. I *knew* that hungry, lonely student world of lowest-class living: Did Wystan ever know it?

Wystan's conversation at home was often a valuable tutorial, as when I dropped a casual remark about Robert Frost's poem "Neither out Far nor in Deep." Wystan had challenged me to recite all the poem from memory, and as I did so in meditative rhythm, Wystan leaned back in his chair, puffing Olympian smoke at our local ceiling. Finishing, I ventured, "It has a timeless silhouette quality."

"Yes!" Wystan went one better: "It's a kind of epic poem, isn't it?"

At that very moment I might have told him how much I admired his *On This Island,* a lyric masterpiece with epic qualities in a "whole view," impersonal and apart from Frost's bit of seaside philosophy—a modern "far out" poem with global sweep, related to Matthew Arnold's "Dover Beach," yet retaining social significance and a social challenge, the essence of Wystan's best early poetry. But it wasn't in the nature of our friendship for me to applaud Wystan's poems to his face, nor would he condone it.

Frost figured in our conversation a few times, but when I praised Stephen Spender's early poem "I think continually of those who were truly great," Wystan froze, unwilling to discuss a peer's poem, just as he'd declined to discuss Dylan Thomas in our first talk in Brinnin's Book Room. And he might conclude almost any talk with tutorial advice: "If you want to understand English poetry, study Pope." When I conveyed my respect for Day-Lewis, MacNeice, and MacDiarmid, Wystan said, "Really, now, you can't afford to miss Hardy." And once he warned me, "As an American, you must look into James's *American Scene*."

When students came to our at-homes, Wystan was pleased, but he wasn't when so few of them came to confer with him in his tiny university office (distinguished by a file card on which he'd scribbled, "I inhabit this hole from two to four on Thursdays, W. Auden"). We discussed some of the students, and one lunchtime Wystan perplexedly read to me a letter: "Mr. Auden, I can't let my twenty-first birthday pass without apologizing for the rude manner in which I responded to your comments on *Don Quixote* . . ." Wystan wagged his head over the handwritten note. "Dear me! Really, I can't recall *any* student's rudeness, much less his."

Wystan showed me a paper written by a student whom I recall as most quiet and attentive in class. The paper was written in faint ink with nine or ten words on the beginning line, but each succeeding line was shorter, until the last line had only three words. Wystan waved his hand over the wedge-shaped writing and decreed, "This person needs help! Whatever can be wrong with him?"

At home Wystan often deplored students' low literacy, declaring, "They just might learn correct English, and how to write it!" I mentioned my favorite Northwestern University professor, Frederick Faverty, who would announce to his classes, "When you take my literature courses, you're obliged to speak and write good English, or else take a makeup course in grammar and composition." Wystan grunted, in Oxford accent, his approval.

Wystan didn't go to movies in the autumn of 1941, but he spoke of his old favorites, *The Maltese Falcon, The Thirty-Nine Steps,* and all of Marlene Dietrich's films. He shrugged at my praise for *Childhood* of Maxim Gorki (of which I'd said, "To see the Gorki film is to see why the Russian Revolution had to happen"). We spoke of my favorite Flaherty films, and Wystan mentioned some documentaries he'd worked on.

Sometimes Wystan imitated Marlene Dietrich's singing and speaking style, and once he sat at the kitchen table while I prepared dinner (a time and a ritual he liked), a Dietrich record echoed from the living room. Wystan slouched back in his chair, his face turned up toward the cigarette smoke cloud he was creating, while he echoed Dietrich's last husky love-whisper, "Johnnie!"—pronounced in Dietrich style, "Chonnie!"—as he exhaled in a sexually satisfied postorgasmic manner. Often while taking his first twilight drink of the day, he would bawl out a Dietrich song, "Seeee whaaat th' buoys in th' baackroom are haaafing / And tell them I vill haaaff th' saaame!"

Cabaret songs echoed from Wystan's record player, including a French one, "Sisters, Don't Love Sailors," and Wystan oddly (or queerly) chanted the phrase, omitting the comma. In such songs, in limericks, and in opera arias, Wystan sought a wide range, just as he sought variety in literature and in individual Americans.

When the first melty snow fell through leafless trees, Wystan gazed at the white-coated garden: "It reminds me of the north of England." We both hurried to our work desks, early. In such wintry moments I was supersensitive to the cozy luxury of our home, and I was conscious of Robert Frost's lively ghost on Pontiac Trail. Once when I went down into the basement for fireplace logs, I looked at the rough stone walls and thought, "These are the mortared stones which Frost saw when he came down here for wood, coal, or cider." But that was a chance thought, for neither Wystan nor I mentioned to anyone that the new house stood on the cellar walls of the old house in which Frost had once lived.

My journal notes:

> In class, Wystan gave a spirited appreciation of the Marx Brothers' films, and I sat there on the hard oak seat, aware that their crazy world is far from my fictional world of Michigan farmland and farmers. Although I can share W's enthusiasm for the Brothers, it's hard for me to relate my world to theirs. Wystan relates to them easily.

I think that Wystan wanted the Marx Brothers to romp through the class's routine, to enrich it; but some of his students told me they were baffled at his embrace of the Marx in plural—and especially baffled were those who were on guard against Marx the singular, even though Wystan seemed to have forgotten the latter. I urged such students to observe Wystan "at home" and learn that he was inclined to join the Marx Brothers, if they would have him, as well they might.

Wystan's boyish clowning, his love of play and sense of humor, his affection for limericks and puns, his taste for sentimental and traditional song, his appetite for frothy and witty fiction (such as that by Ivy Compton-Burnett, whom he loved to quote) was evidence of his hunger to live on various levels. When he stood or paced before his attentive class in Angell Hall, making light of *Othello* or making fun with the Marx Brothers, none of us had time to think of Wystan's world fame and achievements or of the prophetic themes of his major work, for he came to teach us world literature, especially his favorite exemplary authors.

During a quiet at-home moment a woman student abruptly asked Wystan, "What made Yeats so important to you, as he appears to be in the 'Yeats' poem?" And Wystan, plainly taken by surprise, lifted his trusty cigarette in defense, sank back into the wing chair, and mumbled, "I, uh, believe that it's true, that is, one must—really!—learn to praise, uh, when one feels compelled to do so!" He was embarrassed at being forced to provide an instant but honest evaluation of his poem. After this intrusion the air cleared (less the tobacco smoke), and the evening proceeded on its homey, low-key course.

In class, during at-homes, or on the lecture platform in those days, Wystan seldom uttered witty or memorable phrases, being generally earnest and intense. He enjoyed "just talking," and did a lot of it. He enjoyed jokes of any kind, puns, parables, and any nice turn of speech; and though he was a chuckler, a chortler (in later years, something of a grunter), he loved to provoke or be provoked into a laugh. A belly laugh was an occasion "devoutly to be desired."

At the home of Albert and Angelyn Stevens, Wystan met James Rettger, a university instructor who was writing a book in a private language, and Wystan enthused about the project, reading some of the manuscript pages to me. I recall my dis-appreciation, but Wystan orated, "An invented language is a form of poetry, for it's obliged to *name* everything, to create and populate a new universe. Fascinating!"

In my naturalist mood I objected: "Such writing results in phonetic music, not literature. Literature is a means of cultural communication, and Rettger's writing communicates only interesting sounds. Besides, Joyce in *Finnegans Wake* . . ."

Wystan cut me off: "Never mind Joyce! Rettger com-municates through a music of his own, which I happen to find fascinating."

Jimmy and Esther Rettger were a lively young couple with children; and their cottage household near the Ar-boretum was a welcome addition to Wystan's small list of friendly homes until Jimmy left town, taking his invented language along with him to the State Department in Washington, where he became a wartime recruit in cryptology.

One day Wystan told me that a student in his class, Bob Hemenway, was coming to dinner, and this pleased us both, for Bob was intellectual, sensitive, and what used to be called well-bred, a most attractive fellow whom one had to like at sight. The evening of the dinner I was late in arriving home, for I'd left my Plymouth at a Saline garage for repairs and hitchhiked the twelve miles to Ann Arbor, shopped for groceries, and walked the last mile loaded with heavy bags. I was weary enough, but even wearier when Wystan greeted me with: "Really, now! Do you happen to know what time it is?" It was my habit in those days not to tell Wystan why I was late, but I could sympathize with his concern while I hastened to prepare the dinner. It wasn't my fault that Wystan thought groceries grew on trees outside the kitchen.

At six-fifty Wystan came into the kitchen and talked to himself while taking plates from the cupboard: "Let's see, now . . . hmmm, *two* plates, *two* soup spoons," and so on through the place settings, even though I'd gotten the message with the first "two." Standing by the hot broiler I flushed even redder, annoyed with Wystan's roundabout way of telling me that he wanted to dine alone with Bob. As I prepped the rissole potatoes I could envision myself serving a series of young guests, to each of whom I felt superior. My face was hot with the cool puritanical suspicion that Wystan had invited a sexual prospect; however, not knowing Hemenway, I was mistaken.

Within the hour I prepared and served the dinner and went to my room with a little glass of Pinot Noir to toast my contented solitude. From the living room I heard predictable opera records and a murmur of voices; but at nine o'clock there was a commotion in the hallway and Wystan's urgent tones, followed by the unmistakable noise of Hemenway vomiting in the bathroom. On the landing I faced a worried Wystan who said, sotto voce, "The beef kidneys were too rich for Bob." I answered guiltily, "Yes, and boiled potatoes would have been better than rissoles." Beyond us, the meal was gone for sure, in wholehearted, whole-bellied upheaval. All of it. The rich black coffee, the affable Pinot Noir, the Liederkranz cheese, and the aquamarine grapes: too much for a high-strung student. Wystan soon took Hemenway home, and I was left to ponder our only gourmet calamity.

Days later my journal notes:

Wystan at lunch: "You know Hemenway? Something dreadful happened. He came up to me in Angell Hall, stammering, 'Now, don't get me wrong,' and 'Please don't think that I uh . . .' and so on. It seems that he didn't know about *me* and that he told a few persons about being here for dinner, and vomiting, until they said, 'Of course—Wystan has designs on you!' Heaven knows that I have no more designs on Bob Hemenway than I have on the man in the moon. If people are going to talk like *that*, I daren't have *anyone* up here for dinner.

"And what must they be saying about you, Charlie? People are free to say that I'm queer, for heaven knows that I am, but when they begin saying that everyone around me is queer, why, it just makes it impossible to live here!"

So. Vile town tongues are working overtime, but even I had suspected that Bob was being solicited. My ignorance. So I must put on my fresh new awareness of evil, ordered by Wystan Auden, and admit that provincial Ann Arbor is slavering at the Achilles' heel of our distinguished poet.

My October 1941 journal notes:

Wystan ponders some of my old journal entries on family horrors, parricide, suicide, and incest, and he shrugs, "To be expected in such a family." Again, "Eventually, Charlie, you'll fall in love with someone like your mother, with her strength, her talkativeness, her humor, but with a heart full of love rather than hate. You, Charlie, have more hate in you than you

[49]

realize, but your mother loves you more than she loves others in your family because you rebelled, which the others daren't do. And you do have affection for people . . ."

Again, "The wish for your father's death was present in you, as well as in the others, though you can't admit it. The son's wish to replace the father is universal, an impulse to occupy the place of responsibility. It's a natural wish and you must accept it."

I couldn't accept it, but Wystan was proceeding with my destiny:

"Your life could make good fiction, Charlie, but when you write it, don't forget to emphasize spiritual aspects. Make your terrible family scenes lead from one to the other towards the Grecian climax. Why *do* so many young writers go on and on about sunsets and landscapes when they should be writing significantly about human feelings."

At breakfast one October morning Wystan asked, "What did you and your girlfriend do last night?"

"Well," I began, sheepishly, "I feel guilty about one thing I did."

"Yes? Guilty?"

"Yeah," I murmured, my head cocked toward the cooking eggs, "I, uh, read some of my verses to her . . ."

"Hahahahaha!" he roared, and roared again, head back. "I know *just* how you feel—guilty!" And he was off again, in the loudest belly laugh I'd heard from him. "Well," he said finally, while I glanced at his wet eyes and fox-toothy grin, "well, Charlie, did it work?"

"Somewhat," I admitted, modestly.

One day Wystan sat down to lunch in the kitchen, saying, "Charlie, I heard those awful oaths out here. What happened?"

"Oh, I had a skillet of perfectly fried potatoes by the

broiler, but when I lifted the tray of sweetbreads, down went the potatoes onto the floor."

"Hmmm. Too bad. But it didn't hurt the delicious potatoes."

"The hell it didn't! I kicked 'em under the stove."

"Dear me, don't. The floor is clean enough to eat from, you know. One eats a certain amount of bacteria . . ."

"Wystan! The floor is *not* clean enough to eat from."

"Really, it looks clean, it hasn't any shit on it."

"Well, it almost has."

"Uh huh! So you've been shitting on it?" he bantered, doggedly eating refried leftover noodles. "Heaven knows, the floor is quite clean."

"Not through any effort of yours!" I finished, even while I chuckled at the way he'd pronounced, moistly, "de-lish-shus potatoes," his favorite food floored.

Wystan mailed letters from the house or from the branch post office in Nichols Arcade near the campus, sometimes borrowing stamps from me (always repaying me promptly), but he liked aerogram forms or plain postal cards, and he liked to get his letters directly from the postman's hand at the door, as is the custom even today in some parts of the British Isles. But our American letter carriers don't ring doorbells customarily, so if Wystan heard the wooden lid of the mailbox clunk shut in mid-morning, he'd stride out to claim the mail, ripping open certain letters, reading while ambling back to his work table, and often reading me parts of letters from Chester, who wrote fairly faithfully. Some letters were reread over luncheon coffee; none were discarded in my presence but were kept on his night table for later discarding.

Wystan might pick up the phone in the entryway to call anyone anytime anywhere on a literary point. His incoming calls were remarkably brief, Wystan offering a few pithy words, such as, "Perhaps that *is* a good idea—I'll think about it," and then hanging up. If by chance it was an invitation, of which there were few, he'd say, "*So* nice of you to invite me. Thanks. See you there!" and hang up. Once he got a midnight call from Los Angeles: "Really now! I don't know what time you have out there, but it's nighttime here and I'm going back to bed," hanging up on the last word. Not rudely, but with the determination of a private poet who guarded his private hours.

Once at 1223 Wystan answered the phone, spoke three or four words, hung up, and turned to me, saying, "So far, my agent in New York has done me no good except for selling serial rights of 'New Year Letter' to the *Atlantic Monthly*."

The telephone never could capture Wystan as long as he could hang up. Although Chester sometimes made long phone calls to Wystan late in the evening, there was never a marathon talk.

One day Wystan got a phone call concerning the then innovative manuscript collection at the University of Buffalo, which he had visited; he gave me his favorable impressions of the manuscript and letter collection there, but ended somberly: "I wonder what effect this American mania for collecting manuscripts will have on American writers? It's bound to have a bad effect on *some* writers, making them even more self-conscious, perhaps influencing them to write in a manner agreeable to collectors rather than to their muse."

In 1941, manuscript, holograph, and authors' archive collections were quietly housed in some university libraries, as well as in the Library of Congress; but few persons, Wystan least of all, would have predicted the phenomenal growth of archive collections, such as those at Harvard, Yale, the University of Texas, and the New York Public Library. Were Wystan alive today, I think that he would browse such collections with delight, while disapproving them in self-defense.

I recall that we discussed at the house on Pontiac Trail a popular autobiographical book that revealed the scandalous behavior of some public figures. Wystan, standing by the hearth with the *New York Times* in hand, declared, "Dear me! If people are going to tattle on each other like this, one can't feel free to speak one's mind to anybody, even in private. It's *not* fair!" Yet, in later years Wystan was to publish his enthusiasm for the "tattling" done on Lord Byron in a revealing biography.

FOUR

Seekers after happiness, all who follow
The convolutions of your simple wish,
It is later than you think . . .
"Consider"

"MY WIFE, ERIKA, WILL BE EATING WITH US, BUT SLEEPING ON campus when she comes here to lecture," Wystan told me casually in early October 1941.

I was aware of the prevalent legends concerning Wystan's marriage to Erika Mann, imaginative legends promoted by the literati and by enterprising journalists. First, it was rumored, Erika cabled Wystan in England: "Will you marry me? I must gain British citizenship or be put across the border into Germany, where Hitler will kill me." The cable was reputed to have come from such different places as Luxembourg, France, Switzerland, and Amsterdam. Variations on this legend had Wystan meeting Thomas Mann in England, where Mann asked Wystan to marry Erika, to save her from the Third Reich. In succeeding chapters of this entertaining tale, Erika came to Southampton port, where Wystan married her at dockside and then "eloped" to the Orient (or variously to New York, to Australia, to the Canary Islands) with Christopher Isherwood, while Erika "eloped" to Switzerland with her woman lover.

These charming and flippant legends bear little resemblance to the true story, as related by Isherwood in *Christopher and His Kind*: In 1935, in Amsterdam, Erika asked Christopher (a British subject) to join her in a "passport marriage" so that she could acquire British citizenship and thus be free to live outside the reach of the Third Reich; but Christopher refused, for family reasons, and passed the proposal by letter to Wystan in England, who wired back, "Delighted." The couple were married in Herefordshire, and Erika was safe from the Reich, which had declared her "an enemy" of her homeland because of her anti-Nazi activities. The damning part of the false legends is that all of them stressed the romantic rather than the political. The fact was that Erika's life was in danger and Wystan wanted to save her.

Erika came to tea at 1223 and stayed for dinner, a lively occasion, for the "tea" turned to a fifth of Dant whiskey. Erika was then a handsome woman with black hair, dark eyes, and swarthy skin; and I for one appreciated her outfit of browns and bronze, her bangles, bracelets, and chain necklaces. She looked—and sounded—like a slim, fancy gypsy. Her manner was hearty, if correct, while Wystan was strenuously polite, flushed with tea and whiskey as well as the challenge of hosting this female ball of fire.

Erika looked at me often while speaking to Wystan as we three sat before the fire. Her dark eyes shone with excitement while she recounted her interview with Rudolf Hess; she claimed to be the first German national to speak with him following his sensational parachute drop onto British soil. Erika believed Hess to be "innocent" and "sincere" in his quest to end the war with Great Britain, even though no British authorities concurred with her belief. Erika spoke English with a hefty German accent and periodically backtracked in German, with Wystan responding in German and Erika waving a jingling wrist at me, "Exchoose me! So sorry I do *thadt!*" then explaining in ponderous English what she'd said in German.

I prepared a roast beef dinner, and Wystan carved the beef into English-style slivers until Erika demanded "won beeg theek slice, wif crust, puleeze!" We all ate like Michigan lumberjacks, and Wystan drank too much whiskey and wine as he tried to cope with Erika's flood of words; but the good food and black magic of black coffee toned down the words at last, and at ten I left Wystan and Erika talking more softly in German before the burning logs.

During her several days in and out of 1223, Erika was often alone with me and told me (as Elizabeth Mayer did later on) that Wystan appreciated my nature and capabilities; so adroit was Erika's approach that I hardly realized that she was giving me the Pitch, in nearly incomprehensibly accented English: "Huf course, Vystan egg-spects thad you vill stay mif heem h'allvays, so thad you bofth vill haff a huome, vwhere to wride and liff!" I attended her pitch but replied that neither Wystan nor I could foresee the future.

Erika gave her one lecture in the Women's League auditorium to a university audience that listened attentively to her warnings of the holocaust already gripping Europe. Although her lecture was carefully loaded with Germanic cognates, and well coached by German-English advisors, it was heavy going for any listener unaccustomed to such heavy German accents. In this way, Erika resembled her father, Thomas Mann, who gave many American lectures that were understood by very few American listeners. However, her reception was a social success, admirers crowding around Erika, while Wystan stood beside her and shook as many hands as were proffered, proud to be the husband of a distinguished anti-Fascist activist.

Standing nearby, I didn't hear one person ask Wystan about his own writing or his own European experiences, much less invite him to a faculty or town home for tea. It was Erika's show, not his, and I knew that he suffered as an émigré from the embattled Europe for which Erika crusaded.

How happy Wystan would be next day, alone at work on his Christmas oratorio!

"Those who wish, may come to my house on Thanksgiving Day from two to four. We shall play records of *Parsifal* and discuss it over tea," Wystan announced to his class.

[55]

Five students came, including a lonely Nisei, and *Parsifal* swelled through the rooms. The hearth flamed in defiance of a chilly gray sky beyond the big window, but our mood was melancholy. I served tea as cheerfully as possible after a difficult session with my writing, and I was sensitive to the lush smells coming from the kitchen, where a stuffed bird roasted, but not for these students who sniffed it. No discussion of *Parsifal* occurred, and when Wystan showed the laconic group out the door into the sunless chill, kitchen odors nagged their nostrils as they turned toward whatever festivity they could find in dorms and rooming houses, or, alas, in local hashhouses. They were desolate as I had been in other years, far from any holiday home, and I mooned after them.

Wystan came into the kitchen with a bottle of Pinot Noir to cure his own desolation, and while he sat and talked I tended the dinner. My journal notes:

> On Thanksgiving we tippled and toasted, and enjoyed a few laughs, which I'd thought impossible during the haunted day. Wystan asked and I told about a breadline Thanksgiving in my Depression Chicago, and I described my dollar-a-week reformed coalbin room in a Northside basement, my epic long marches in search of subsistence work, and the personal humiliation of hunger and poverty. "Here's to now!" said Wystan, lifting a shot of Erika's whiskey. While we washed dishes Wystan recited Lear and Carroll, and bawled out a few Berlin cabaret ditties. But I was early to bed with an awareness of icy wind rushing around the house, flowing into the wake of one more bachelor holiday.

After Thanksgiving, Benjamin Britten arrived with Peter Pears and Elizabeth Mayer for a stay, their enthused voices filling the house, Wystan smiling happily to have them under his roof. "Benjy" conducted Peter a cappella in the Britten-Rimbaud "Illuminations," Peter's erotic tenor seeming to swell the rooms. Elizabeth was handsome and stately, a European presence, her brown hair silver-laced, braided and coiled into a crown; her queenly bosom shook with laughter as she chummed with us four raucous males. She took me aside and said: "Wystan values you, Charles. Not only for your practical talents, but for your character. Stay with him! You'll always have a home, your writing will prosper. He's not difficult to live with. I know! He lived with us." I nodded, attentive but noncommittal.

Benjy was pale and youthful with English indoor grace, his face with its half-smile turned to his friends, who did most of the talking. Peter, handsome and irrepressible, loomed large over his Benjy, and I didn't need Wystan to tell me, as he did in a murmured aside, "Now there's a happily married couple."

Eating, drinking, and talking for three long days, rushing about town in the green Pontiac, visiting Wystan's friends, the group still had time to appreciate my American attempt at British savories. We all washed dishes together, and they explained their jokes. Yet, when they left for New York, like a warm wind rushing eastward, I appreciated our quiet, creative house as never before.

> *Sophomores and peasants,*
> *Poets and their critics*
> *Are the same in bed.*
> "Heavy Date"

At the kitchen window Wystan watched snowflakes ticking leafless trees and asked, "Charlie, do you know Professor B——? No? I do believe that he's queer—quite queer!—and doesn't know it."

A day or so later, Wystan declared cheerfully, "Dear me, I do feel *queer* today." I had nothing to offer, for—alas—I felt quite otherwise, even while I observed that Wystan appeared no more or less queer than usual; but I was interested to note that he used the word "queer" in private and "homosexual" in public and at-homes, although he used neither in his classes. I recall his first forthright "I am a homosexual man," in a time when such assertions were rare. When he used the word "queer" he pronounced it clearly, but his "dear" had an r so soft it sounded like "deah" to me; and I heard it often, for to English Wystan, almost everybody was a "deah" until proven otherwise.

In those years I heard working people and students use "queer," but rarely "homosexual," which then sounded more clinical than colloquial; a few used "fairy," as in "fairy nice" men, and fewer used "frail," applied to both men and women; but none, in my recollection (or in my journal), used "gay," which came into more popular usage after the fifties. Later I noticed that Wystan described himself in his early *Letters from Iceland* as "gay," but in his first years in America I hardly heard him use that word in conversation, just as I never heard him use a British "bloody."

One morning Wystan received a letter on elegant stationery, and he read it to me while he paced about the room. The letter writer expressed admiration for Wystan's poetry and asked to meet him to discuss poetry.

"I do believe this person may be queer," declared Wystan, turning the fancy page over and over in his hand, examining it, sniffing it, in his lonely search for others of his own kind.

I understood Wystan's loneliness, for it was related to my own, especially during the thirties when I rode freight trains or slept in hobo "jungles" near the tracks, the chilly western skies overhead and no friend or family member knowing where I was or if I was still alive. Mine had been a celibate loneliness. And when I went to my celibate bed at 1223 Pontiac I was aware of the first wintry winds swaying leafless trees out in the garden, our chimney smoke whisked away into a cold sky above the stone-dotted cemetery just up the street. I was grateful for the comfort of the studio house that sheltered two distinct and individual "lonelies."

Perhaps the roses really want to grow,
The vision seriously intends to stay;
If I could tell you I would let you know.
　　　　　　"If I Could Tell You"

Caroline Newton, Wystan's affluent friend who gave him carte blanche to buy books and records on her charge accounts, came to stay with us, sleeping in Wystan's room while he slept on a cot in the basement. In a few days Caroline discovered Wystan's sacrifice of his room, and she declared, "I'm leaving soon. I had no idea the house was so small. I can't bear to inconvenience Wystan, so I shall leave." And leave she did, after several days.

Caroline directed monologues at me, enthusing over Wystan's poetry. "Charles, you know that Wystan's Notes to 'New Year Letter' have made literary history!" And much more of the same, with her proofs of Wystan's greatness. I was able to tease her: "But Caroline, Wystan hasn't cleaned the house as he promised to do!" Caroline evidently didn't understand my teasing; she handed me a copy of Wystan's villanelle "If I Could Tell You," which Wystan had given her at lunch. I had seen it in the little magazine *Vice Versa*, and was interested in the strict form, which recalled to me Wystan's firm remark to his class on classical verse forms: "Poetic form is, uh, a challenge to prove that what the poet has to say is not, uh, an accident." What Wystan has to say in this villanelle is almost pure cliché, but the form and the musical repetition produce a poetic spell of magic; and when we hear magic we aren't inclined to weigh it, nor can we measure it with calipers: a song has had us.

Caroline was raving: "Wystan is incredible! This great poem was published in a tiny magazine—don't ask me why. It could have been published anywhere."

"Well, Caroline, it *was* published somewhere, so . . ." But Caroline was drawing her plump figure as tall as possible, wiping her graying hair back from her young spinster brow, as she intoned, "This poem is—*Immortality!*—in eighteen lines!" I put the poem onto the kitchen table, murmuring, "Well, it's a good poem." It reminded me of Heine's sentiment, his bittersweet irony, but I said, staring at Caroline's calligraphy, "This looks so much like Wystan's handwriting," and Caroline got off her immortality cloud and said, with a sheepish smile, "Oh yes, I just can't help it."

When Wystan returned to the house at dusk, Caroline issued onto the landing, cooing, "Wystan! Oh, Wystan, the poem is bee-oo-ti-fooool! Wystan, do come here to me, please!"

Wystan, seeming to pale under his usual pallor, and afraid to be cornered in the entry or living room, came into the kitchen, slammed the door, and sat behind it, visibly shaken, and protesting in his preachiest, English-offended tone, "This is *too* much! It's absurd." Caroline cooed again from the upper landing, and Wystan went to the back door, opening it, ready to fly; but she went back to her room, and Wystan sat staring at me with angry eyes, his face working: "One must *nevah* carry on in such a manner over a poem. Ridiculous! One has only to say, 'I like it,' or 'I don't like it.' And that's that." He sat watching me intently, as he sometimes did, and watching my cooking, for him a spectator sport. "Now, Charlie, I'd like you to read some short pages. Have you time now?"

I had. Agreeably, I turned off the stove burner.

"I'll fetch them." He stepped across the hall to the living room, returning at once with typed pages of "Songs for Saint Cecelia," as he then titled them.

I sat at the kitchen table, reading the songs carefully, while Wystan watched me for a moment and then went to the living room, closing the door. When he returned later, he asked, with touching eagerness, "Well, now?" And I said, self-consciously, "I, uh, liked them!"

Wystan looked keenly at me, nodded acceptance of my casual tone, and gathered up the pages from the table, handling them with rough familiarity. "That's all one wants to know!—if the work is liked, or not."

I wanted to believe Wystan, but I felt guilty in not spouting some enthusiasm. After all, I was the founder and Secretary of the Poetry Club! But Wystan sat down and puffed twilight clouds of Lucky smoke, squinting at his floating creations, and saying, "By the way, did that phrase, 'O lift your little pinkie, / And touch the winter sky,' connote anything, uh, sexual?"

"Nope. I took 'pinkie' to be a hand. Charming."

"Hmm, can 'pinkie' signify 'penis' to Americans?"

"Perhaps, but not to me." I continued cooking.

Before dinner, Wystan told Caroline in neutral but firm tones that he didn't like anyone to make a fuss over his poems; one ought to say only if the poems were liked or not. Caroline took this in good grace, and that was that.

During Caroline's week-long visit, she came to Wystan's Thursday class and sat in the front row with me, very much the attentive student, confiding, "I do hope Wystan will talk on Shakespeare. That would be so great!"

No one, not even Wystan, ever knew what Wystan would talk about, but at home he had talked to me one evening about Shakespeare: "When a director seeks an actor to play the role of Hamlet, he may as well go out on the street and take the first person who comes along. Because the role doesn't require an actor. One has only to recite Hamlet's speeches, which are instructions and arguments to himself on how to act the roles he decides to play." In one autumn class, Wystan had rambled extensively through *Othello*; and in a later year I was to hear him tackle Shakespeare in a New York lecture.

But now Wystan was talking about Cervantes, rambling and digressing, as he often did. Discussing the role of inspiration in writers, he slowly paced the floor before the class in gangly slow motion and said, to my astonishment: "Recently I had the rare luck of watching a member of this class perform on ice skates. He did the most unbelievable dance on skates. I should say that he was inspired to skate that way. Uhmmm, yes, he had inspiration." (And I thought I'd been having just a regular workout on ice.) Caroline turned to look right at me, and though my head didn't turn, my color did. After class she said, "It must feel wonderful to be recognized in such a way."

And I answered that I'd rather be recognized for writing a good poem.

On the first Sunday in December, Wystan and Caroline were dining out, so I spent the day visiting my next oldest brother (not one of my "evil" brothers) at nearby Northville, where he was founding a tree and plant nursery. It was fairly balmy for December, and I was glad to be outdoors under a wide sky on tawny fields dotted with evergreens, symbolic of John's hopeful future. He was still building and improving his household, so that at dusk we were hammering, sawing, and boarding up a little outhouse. At twilight I was relaxing with John and his Elva in their two-room cottage when suddenly the radio began to bark out news from Pearl Harbor: Japanese air squadrons had virtually destroyed our Hawaiian outpost. "Now we're in it," said John quite calmly. We talked soberly about the war and wartime realities until I went home.

At breakfast on Monday, Wystan was war-worried but assumed an unruffled manner: "Really, it's about what we expected, isn't it?" Our long breakfast was broken only by Wystan's taking coffee up to an indisposed Caroline; then we continued our Monday morning quarterbacking of the Hawaiian disaster. Frowning, planting his elbows on the kitchen table, Wystan recounted memories of other wars and concluded, "By the way, Charlie, where were you when Hitler's Germans invaded Poland?" Wystan's readers knew that he wrote in his poem "September 1, 1939"—"I sit in one of the dives/ On Fifty Second Street." He was waiting for love while he scribbled passionate stanzas that challenged mankind to battle "negation and despair," to "Show an affirming flame." As for me, I was sweating on horsedrawn wagons in a vast wheat field near Sherman, South Dakota, along with other harvest "stiffs." We were expecting the big noon meal to be brought to us when a truck came hurtling over the golden stubblefield, sluing to a stop as bearded farmers leapt out yelling, "War! War! The Germans are in Poland."

"And what did the men do?" Wystan asked.

"Do? The farmers jumped for joy! They danced with

each other, let out Indian war whoops—'Good old war! Now we'll get a good price for grain.' "

"And so they did," said Wystan gravely. I was ashamed of the farmers, but Wystan was already making comments on economics as a cause of war; he judged that few persons realized the true causes of any given war and that only its victims realized the true horror of it. We talked part of the morning, until Wystan drove downtown to return with every available newspaper. We both read them, our coffee klatch continuing until lunch time. The Detroit and local newspapers were wild and vengeful, even though they printed mostly background material on the Japanese armed forces, our navy, and the probable course of the war. There was much conjecture as to where the Japanese would attack us again and if the other Axis powers, Germany and Italy, would launch surprise attacks. Perhaps New York and San Francisco would be shelled! History had us in her nervous hands.

"You *know*, Charlie, gasoline rationing will certainly follow. And our green Pontiac could be confiscated! Maybe we should deck it out with American flags. Where can we buy a stars-and-stripes insignia? We might have red, white, and blue plaques painted all over the Pontiac. The authorities wouldn't confiscate such a patriotic motor!"

I joined Wystan in defensive laughter and made another pot of coffee.

"Seriously, Charlie, I must volunteer! Every one of us must help our nation. You know, I'd like to get into the submarine service—it's such a challenge to fate! If a bomb hits a sub, you all go down together." He puffed his cigarette, his face sad and pensive, then turned to see how I took his announcement. I weathered it, knowing that he suffered guilt at being away from his own embattled Britain and was anxious to prove his loyalty to his new nation.

Familiarity with world tragedy breeds acceptance, and within a day Wystan was saying, "We must carry on as best we can," which meant that our lives weren't going to change very radically very fast.

My journal notes:

Snow is falling, falling, beginning to cover the skin
of soot on our flat roof, and scratching pens echo the
sporadic tapping of Wystan's portable typewriter. Art
itches itself in this little house. We know that awful
days await us. More ships will be sunk, more towns
and cities leveled while troops march up gang planks
of transports, men moving into death's open jaws.
Slowly we serve our tiny roles in time's riddle.

Caroline said that she would "carry on" through her remaining days with us and conferred with me over the "surprise
dinner" she planned for Wystan: vichyssoise, sirloin steak—
the finest of everything. We drove to Witham's excellent wine
cellar near the Engineering Arch for spirits. Mr. Witham
emerged from his office, and we had fun selecting Wystan's
favorite Pinot Noirs plus Irish whiskey and a case of French
champagne, all proudly loaded into my Plymouth.

The dinner was a great success, but the honored poet was
offended that such a fuss was being made at a time of world
crisis. Even the ancient bottle of nineteenth-century brandy
that Caroline had brought with her from New York failed to
cheer our gloomy Wystan. But he was cheered by the fact that
Caroline was leaving, and he was delighted that Caroline had
a surprise gift for me.

Wystan had suggested, weeks before, that he and I drive
the green Pontiac to California to spend the Christmas vacation with the Thomas Manns. "Christopher will be there, and
many others. It will be a reunion, it'll be fun once we get
there, and you can explain America to me as we cross it!" But
I didn't want to travel west; I had my heart set on Manhattan,
where some of my friends lived and where all Midwestern
literati went for holidays, as on a pilgrimage.

Wystan respected my plans. He told Caroline I was going
to Manhattan, and she graciously offered me the "surprise"—
a key to her penthouse apartment on the East River in the
mid-50s.

My trip to Manhattan was a success, I met many of
Wystan's friends whom he had suggested I see, including

James and Tania Stern, Chester Kallman's father, Jean Connolly, and Jack Barker. Caroline's apartment, with its original Blake artworks, a table from Samuel Johnson's coffee house, and a glassed terrace overlooking Manhattan, was a treat and a delight to this Midwest student poet. Caroline was at her Pennsylvania estate, and her maid looked in on my comfort every day or so, but I left the city with a large lump in throat: I was resolved to go back to Michigan and work on a farm as a pacifist contribution to the war effort.

Meantime, Wystan had a less pleasing time in California, as he told me later, and he spoke harshly of the Thomas Manns: "At least *they* have all the money they can use," adding, "A-a-act-ually, Charlie, you got the best vacation by going to New York." Peering at me over his teacup, Wystan said puckishly, "At the Manns', we took turns screwing a friend on Thomas's big bed when the family was away."

Viva California.

FIVE

I cannot see a plain without a shudder:
"O God, please, please, don't ever
make me live there!"
"Plains"

WYSTAN WAS STILL IN CALIFORNIA WHEN I RETURNED TO ANN
Arbor after New Year's 1942, and I left him a note: "I got a
job on a farm in nearby Dexter. Will miss the life here." Packing all my worldly belongings in cartons and thrift shop suitcases, I stacked them in the little garage whose door was ever
open to Michigan weather. A few days later, still staggering
from a draft board interview and war gloom, I returned to the
house to find Wystan at work in the living room and we sat by
the hearth to talk.

"At the very least, Charlie, you may keep your room here
and commute to the farm," Wystan said.

"Can't do it, Wystan. We're up at four A.M. and out to
the barns. We're through work at eight P.M., when I fall onto
my attic cot. No time for commuting."

Wystan pursed his lips. "Don't act the fool. Draft boards
aren't taking university students, so you'll be safe here until
June."

"Nope. Can't do it," I insisted.

I went out to the garage to load all my junk into the
Plymouth, but Wystan was at my heels, angry, using a tone I

was never to hear again: "No, you don't, Charlie! I won't stand for it. You fetch those things right back into the house. You say you have a tiny attic room at the farm, but there's plenty of room here. Now! You may get a draft deferment and be back here before the end of the month. No! I won't have your things out here in the damp garage where rain and snow will get at them!" He spoke rapidly, waving a hand as if he wanted to slap me while my mind idiotically repeated his odd pronunciation of "garage," like "gay-raazhze."

We faced each other in the cold air while dusk closed around us, lumpy cartons of my anarchic past piled between us. We stared silently at each other, each of us obsessed with separate and selfish thoughts. Then Wystan gave a nervous growl—a half-sob—and stooped to seize a carton and strode with it into the house. Reluctantly I followed with another carton, and in a few trips we had all my belongings, including Wystan's autographed and annotated books (Ann Arbor's biggest collection), resting in relative safety behind the fireplace wall, Wystan repeating in mollified tones, "I *won't* have your things out there exposed to the *nasty* weather!"

Wystan made tea and served it by the fire, as he had in our first hour in long ago September; but this time we sipped it grimly. When Wystan saw me off with a final, "You just might be back in our home in a few days," I felt better.

But I knew that my life was going off onto its pre-Wystan course, that I'd condemned myself to the snow-heaped hinterland, a local Siberia where my muscles would ache in memory of creative days in a poet's house.

Later I learned that Wystan wrote to Elizabeth Mayer in early January:

> I feel so ashamed at not having written before but I've had one crisis after another. I am completely broke so that I can hardly leave the house. I am losing my cook. My one and only suit has been stolen. In fact, Miss God is being a regular Tartar.
> I do hope Ben and Pete *won't* be able to get away.
> Much love to all.
> Wystan.

Soon after my departure for the farm, Wystan went to visit his friends Albert and Angelyn Stevens, and, as Angelyn told me:

> Wystan came to the door with his overcoat buttoned to the chin, and he sat for some time over the coffee I served him. "Won't you take off your coat?" I asked him. "Uh, nooo, thank you." At last I said as off-handedly as I could, "Do you have a hole in your shirt?"—meaning that I'd mend it for him, as I'd mended other articles for him. But he said, grinning like a boy, "How did you guess it?" and kept his coat on. When he made to leave, Albert went to the door with him and said, "Wystan, do you need some money? We have some we can loan you." But Wystan said, very cheerfully, "Thanks, so much! But, really no."
> Later, Wystan told me and Albert that his suitcase was "stolen" along with other things.

Other things? I wondered, hoping that manuscripts hadn't been stolen, and I guessed that he didn't want my manuscripts, journals, and "things" in the wide-open garage to be stolen, as his had been. At any rate, Wystan was slow to complain to anyone about anything, and, like many an adventurous person, he had bounced over a bad spot, but remained in control, as usual.

At noon on February 4, I drove into Ann Arbor from the nearby farm and parked in the snow on Brooklyn Street where winter sunlight glinted on the buff-colored bricks of the two-story "divinely Victorian house," as Wystan described his new rental to friends. Its many windows looked onto rows of equally respectable houses occupied by academic and professional families. Number 1504 had an entry porch with pretentious turret-dormers rising in front of the second story; there was a tiny patch of front lawn with a larger lawn to the rear, flanked by a small garage; but all Brooklyn Street houses were planted close together, in realtor's harvest fashion. Entering, I faced the varnished oak bannister and to my right a large living room with a happily shabby sofa before a fireplace of green glazed bricks. The time-honored rug, old chairs, lamps, and built-in bookcases had survived an older, calmer academic era. In the many-windowed room to the rear, sunlight spilled over a carved wooden stand holding a huge tome; for this was the house of Thomas A. Knott, general editor of *Webster's New International Dictionary, Second Edition*. Wystan was Prof. Knott's latest lessee.

Wystan came from the dining room, his new work place, to welcome me with a big smile, calling out, *"Chestah!* Come see who's here!" Chester came out of the kitchen, smiling and curious; he appeared as youthful as when I'd first seen him at the New School, two years before. He was wearing new blue jeans, two sizes too big, and a pale blue denim shirt open to his navel. When he shook hands with me, his pale blue eyes gazed carefully into me, and his large moist mouth murmured a casual, "How are you." His light yellow hair was slicked back with water, showing comb marks. Of medium height and well-fleshed but not plump, Chester exuded homey, connubial confidence; with his bare feet thrust into woolly slippers, he slouched and shrugged before Wystan's loving gaze, very much at home.

We all sat in the living room with coffee, and Wystan inquired, "How are things down on the farm?" So I gave him the news—that we were fattening a few thousand spring lambs. Wystan remarked: "A few thousand! Like sheep farms in England." We discussed the war, the times. Chester said scornfully: "You should continue in college. The army won't take you." I assured him that the armed forces wouldn't have a chance of taking me, for I had registered as a conscientious objector and meant it. Chester replied, flicking cigarette ashes: "I can tell you—they're *not* taking me!"

While we sat content over coffee and words, Chester smoked as compulsively and continuously as Wystan; both seemed genial, lazy, a bit tired, Wystan explaining, "Chester arrived only last night, we're still honeymooning." Wystan spoke softly, cocking his head, and Chester smiled indulgently at him.

"Do come around, anytime you get a chance," Wystan said warmly when I left, making me feel relieved, happy for both of them, and grateful that, despite our differences, Wystan and I were still friends.

One February evening, hardened with farm work but soft with sentiment for "other days," I arrived at 1504 Brooklyn Street with a bottle of Pinot Noir, a loaf of potato bread, and a large Liederkranz cheese. It was eightish; Wystan and Chester had dined. "So nice of you to bring us our favorite food!" Wystan enthused, starting for the kitchen with it.

"Wait! Let's have a bite of that bread—I haven't had any for weeks," I said. Chester grabbed the wine bottle: "And I haven't had any wine for half an hour." So I sat at the table by a bowl of seedless white grapes, Wystan brought a knife and plate, and I proceeded with a "bite" of bread smeared with Liederkranz, followed by another and another, Chester and Wystan watching me like a movie, until the entire loaf of bread, most of the cheese, and a half-bottle of wine had gone down my grateful gullet. I sighed contentedly, Wystan brought me a cup of rich black coffee, and I picked grapes from the bowl while we talked idly about almost anything. Later, Wystan referred to this as "the time Charlie brought us bread and cheese, but stayed to eat it all."

"What *did* you eat for supper?" Wystan wondered.

"The regular farm supper! Potatoes fried in leftover grease, slices of baloney, some soured cole slaw, cotton-fluff bread, soupy chocolate pudding, and reboiled coffee. Yum! But they can make a good meal, especially on holidays." And I picked up a last crusty curl of "our" bread, biting it gratefully. Chester put his cigarette aside, stuck his finger in the Liederkranz cheese, smelled it, and licked it thoughtfully, nodding his head vigorously: "Charlie! You know what Liederkranz tastes like? No?" Chester looked at Wystan, and they both laughed teasingly as I shrugged, "I'll settle for plain Liederkranz."

Wystan sat watching the two of us in his old habit of observing others, his face working with passing thoughts.

Finally he said, "Chester, you know that Charlie can cook *anything*. He was excellent, and never had a failure, did you, Charlie? But Chester sometimes has the most *dismal* failures. . . ."

I interrupted: "But I never tried such things as Chester's charlotte russe, or any of his exotic dishes." But Wystan went on, not hearing me, "Chester, what *was* that incredible concoction you flubbed last week?"

"Oh, who knows? *I've* luckily forgotten it," said Chester.

As always with Wystan, I talked about my feelings, and, though the war wasn't a cheerful topic, I confided: "When things are rough at the farm, when I'm stumbling through the snow at four A.M. toward a mountain of cow shit to be shoveled, I'm aware that some Polish or Yugoslavian village is being sacked, women and children murdered, survivors crawling over ice in search of a piece of frozen turnip to eat."

"But I *like* turnips," interrupted Wystan, with mock innocence. "Don't fret over it, Charlie. You're suffering and sacrificing enough." (Later, alone with farm drudgery among hungry cows and sheep, I had wintry solitude in which to reflect on, and to digest, Wystan's words, which were etched, or frosted, on my memory.)

Now, elbows on the table, Wystan was reciting with admiration: "Chester has the most *e-normous* sexual success! As Charlie knows, I didn't find a friend for weeks in Ann Arbor. But Chester gets off the train, takes a cab, and within *minutes* he is getting phone numbers from the cabbie. Chester exudes sex. He never wants for it, wherever he goes!" While Wystan held forth in passionate loyalty, Chester shrugged and smirked in the background. I relaxed at table, returning Wystan's gaze, genuinely happy for their Ann Arbor union. But I knew where I belonged, and I soon left their "comfy" scene for my local Siberia.

Jean-Paul Slusser, Wystan's landlord at Pontiac Trail, sometimes came to Wystan's at-homes on Brooklyn Street, where he once told me, "When I moved into my house after Wystan's departure I discovered in the basement a big brown grocer's bag stuffed with waste paper, that is, typed and hand-written pages of Wystan's corrected manuscripts. There was much illegible scribbling between lines and in the page margins. I took the bag up to the fireplace and burned the whole lot, which I'm told was the wrong thing to do."

When Wystan talked with me on Brooklyn Street, he inquired after my Selective Service "fate," so I described my January appearance before my draft board in Jackson (on the very day I came to 1223 Pontiac Trail to claim my belongings and found Wystan alone). To my stern draft board I had declared that Selective Service officials or armed forces personnel were free to take me out and stand me against a wall to be shot, but no human being could order me to shoot another human being. My reasoning was as clear as my birthright: If person A can order person B (myself) to kill person C (you, or whomever), then human beings will not be able to live together on earth. History proves that, under the principle of state-ordained murder, or war, there is no end to people killing people, but rather an increase in killing, especially of innocent, disinterested women, children, and anyone in state-ordained target zones. War was, and is, my enemy; I had every native, earthly, and personal reason for opposing it, just as Wystan himself had once opposed it.

Wystan and Chester had an extra room at 1504 Brooklyn, which was occupied by Strowan Robertson, a Canadian student of drama at the university and, as he said, "a product of boarding schools." Strowan and Wystan had much in common, including Christianity, and they remained friends for life.

Wystan referred to Chester and Strowan as "my scholarship students," implying that he (or perhaps Caroline Newton) subsidized their studies at the university, but his implication was misleading, for Strowan later wrote to me:

We were scholarship students to the extent that Wystan was interested in us and gave us household duties. Since Chester did the cooking, I was given the laundry chore; that is, getting it listed, bundled and ready for the laundryman to pick up. I told Wystan I'd written my parents that I was a "scholarship student," and he said, "Nonsense, my dear, you're being kept!" I was enormously pleased, "chuffed," as the English say. However, Wystan gave me no money, and no presents except a few books.

Wystan often played the upright piano in the dining room, but when I praised his talent, he pooh-poohed, saying, "Actually, Morgan Forster is the truly impressive keyboard amateur." Wystan played a piano reduction of *Carmen* and sang the Don Jose role; he had the complete *Ring* cycle with Flagstad on records, but liked to substitute Marjorie Lawrence arias for Flagstad when possible.

We had wine by the gallon, and Wystan was the first person I knew who bought cigarettes by the carton. Not only did I start smoking Luckies, but I have bought my cigarettes by the carton ever since. When I rode about Ann Arbor with Wystan in the green Pontiac, he cautioned me not to point out any attractive male on the sidewalk, but inadvertently I once did, and Wystan nearly drove the car off the street toward the ravishing undergraduate.

At Wystan's informal birthday party in February, Strowan and his undergraduate friends danced around the living room where Wystan's albums and singles of old 78 records were lying on the floor near the front windows. From these selected records Wystan would play passages and arias; he warned everyone not to step on the records, but at the height of festivities, Strowan and his young friends were leaping around and over the records, their light fantastic sneaker toes twirling in lively celebration of Wystan's thirty-fifth birthday.

Memories of 1504 Brooklyn were often recounted to me by Strowan in later years:

Some evenings at the house Wystan and Chester read *The Ascent Of F6* aloud, and I thought the choice of roles curious, for Wystan read the part of Ransom, Chester read that of the mother.

In those years we followed a popular comic strip called "Tillie the Toiler," and Tillie once said, "It irks my ilk," which became a pet phrase in our group. Wystan declined things and acts with the excuse, "It irks my ilk." He told me that he had once tried marijuana, and it made his "legs feel as if they were part of a Queen Anne chair," and so he never used it again for it "irked his ilk."

There was a realistic ceramic turd at 1504 Brooklyn, which was first put in my room as a test, then into the refrigerator to startle Chester, and later put under a chair when Esther Rettger brought her infant to the house. Finally it was packaged and mailed to Tom Eliot, who "enjoys scatalogical humor," as Wystan said.

"In the spring of 1942," Strowan continued,

Wystan read passages to me from his typescript of *For the Time Being* and mentioned that he envisioned Sidney Greenstreet in the role of Herod, for he enormously admired Greenstreet in *The Maltese Falcon* film, and in *Across the Atlantic*.

Now, years later, I often think of Wystan sending off sections of *For the Time Being* to "Benjy" Britten, who thought of setting it to music, and how hurt Wystan was when Benjy abandoned the project (though I can't recall exactly when that happened— it might well have been after we all left Ann Arbor). But now I'm glad that Wystan and Benjy's *Paul Bunyan* is rehabilitated, Wystan's lyrics appreciated as they weren't when he wrote them. And I'm happy when Wystan's "Saint Cecelia" with Benjy's music is often broadcast on holiday occasions. . . . "O bless the freedom that you never chose. . . ."

At 1504 I chanted with Chester, at times, "Good little sunbeams," etc., from *The Sea and the Mirror*. I also remember Wystan's severe look when he told me that Prospero's lines, "Just the same, I am very glad that I shall never / Be twenty and have to go through that business again," was written to me.

Those evenings in front of the fire with *Tristan and Isolde*! Wystan could be outrageously repetitive with his Wagner records, but Riesling poured in forgiveness from the gallon jug.

I recall an amusing indiscretion of Wystan's at Hill Auditorium during the Traubel concert in the spring of 1942: she came on stage in a gold lamé "tent." The applause was torrential, but Wystan tried to talk through it, and because I couldn't hear him, he shouted. At that moment, the applause suddenly stopped, and Wystan's unmistakable accent careened throughout the auditorium: "I *must* have that gold frock for Mrs. Rettger's garden party!" In the awful silence, Wystan rendered a rare blush.

Later in the year, while Wystan was lecturing in his Angell Hall classroom, a curious sound reverberated from the campus walkways below the windows, so Wystan opened a window and stuck his head out in order to locate the racket; but he couldn't locate it, so a student came to the window and pointed out children who were pumping along on roller skates, producing the odd noise.

Why should this little incident lodge in my memory? Perhaps because it specifies the general feeling that Wystan was an oddity, an English oddity at that, who was capable of wearing carpet slippers to church!

At one of our costume parties, when some of us dressed up as women (although this was in Chester's apartment after Wystan left Brooklyn Street), Chester infuriated a straight town boy, who then punched his fist through a glass-paned door, cutting himself badly and bleeding all over a first edition of *The Dry Salvages* which Wystan had inscribed and sent to Chester. When Wystan came to Ann Arbor to visit Chester in early 1943, he saw the book and seemed enchanted: "I'll send it back to Tom Eliot. He'll love it!"

Aside from the At Homes, Wystan did little entertaining at 1504 Brooklyn, and I don't recall anyone coming for dinner, except the Stevenses for occasional potlucks, but Donald Elder, a New York editor, came one spring morning, the four of us taking coffee in the garden.

Elder: Wystan, we are publishing Klaus Mann's autobiography.

Wystan: Really. What will you call it?

Elder: We think we'll call it *The Invisible Man*.

Chester: Why not call it *The Subordinate Klaus*?

Wystan guffawed.

Over the years, Strowan confided in me and wrote to me concerning his relationship with Wystan:

It was Wystan who gave me my first true affection for my parents, when I was eighteen. I was invited to dinner and stayed overnight. Wystan, showing me out the front door in the early morning, remarked: "Strowan, you must congratulate your parents for me —they've done a fine job of raising you."

Up to then I never credited my parents with anything, unless it was the usual lack of generosity in family financial matters and their resolute determination to ignore my homosexuality. So, in an important way, Wystan gave my parents to me, and his gift is still operating today, for I confess I sometimes use his line on young men, for whom it has a devastating effect, allowing them to be proud of themselves for what their family did, while they themselves remain innocent of vanity.

During Wystan's spring residence at 1504 Brooklyn, the neighbors' children sensed (or echoed their parents' observation) that the males in Wystan's ménage were "different," and the children soon spoke of them as "a bunch of pansies," as Wystan pensively reported to me. The children believed that Wystan and his ilk sometimes wore women's clothing, so they spied at times through the porch windows and back door, with no known success. Yet Wystan and Chester seemed fairly flattered with the attentions of those neighborhood cherubs.

Before the semester's end, gossip and mild complaints alerted English Department elders to "the possibility that Mr. Auden is too psychologically aberrant for the good of the university community," as one English professor expressed it to me, concluding, "However, our department never got to the point of taking any action on the question of Auden's lifestyle."

Whatever else Wystan did or didn't do in Ann Arbor, he continued "pegging away" on *For the Time Being*, and he completed a full draft of it by June 1942, when he returned to New York, that is, to the East, except for visits to Chester, who stayed on in search of Hopwood Awards—which he never attained—and a university degree, which he did.

May you never be nursed by a grievance,
May your mind approve of your face,
May the odds be in favor of Stevens . . .
"Happy Birthday," unpublished verses to Grace Stevens, 1942

Although Chester was Wystan's greatest personal concern in those days, it was the Stevenses who satisfied Wystan's hunger for "a common American family," as he called them. Albert Stevens was a young professor of English, and his wife, Angelyn, not only mothered their three children but did graduate study, took Wystan's course, and served as a departmental assistant at the university.

It was in October 1941 that Wystan happily waved a note from Angelyn: "Charlie, the Stevenses invite us to dinner! So nice of Angelyn, when no one else cares to invite us. We'll go." We went south of the campus to Marshall Court, a short lane lined with a white picket fence, the Stevenses' dormered bungalow occupying the end of the court. Apples, pears, and grapes perfumed the soft autumn air, colored leaves spangled the side lawn where a cotton clothes line sagged, dotted with wooden pins. On the front porch Wystan stepped carefully over kids' toys, and over a submarine model.

Albert and Angelyn greeted us, introduced us to their children, and we soon sat down to a home-cooked meal, including Angelyn's fresh bread. Albert was slim, self-effacing, and scholarly, as contrasted to his wife, a full-bodied and intense woman, nicely indifferent to personal style in dress, reminding me of some campus refugee housewives. During the meal Angelyn bestowed her reserved but intense little smile on me, confiding, "I'm often late for Mr. Auden's class because of household work and because we have no car. But I do love being in that class." Later, in the kitchen, I noticed typed pages of *The Divine Comedy* pinned above the sink, and Angelyn confessed, "So I can memorize my six cantos of Dante while doing the dishes." As I told Wystan later, quoting Whitman, "The Muse, 'She's here, installed amid the kitchenware!' "

Wystan asked Bradley, aged thirteen, about his interests, and Brad described a physics-chemistry problem he encountered in building a submarine model: he wanted a formula for minerals and chemicals in powder form that would cause his sub to surface from underwater, the X formula being slowly activated in the sub's ballast water until it expelled the ballast and enabled the sub to surface. Wystan attended the enlivened young science student and murmured, "Aaah, two X factors! I'll think about this."

Next day Wystan phoned Brad from home: "Brad, I *think* I have the solution!" And he described it. Years later, Bradley Stevens, designer and inventor, wrote me the details and specifications of the Stevens–Auden sub:

> I recall the autumn evening I showed Wystan Auden the sub, that is, a three-foot wooden hull without its deck, all open in order to permit installation of motors, ballast valves and diving controls which existed only in my mind. I explained to Wystan how the spring-powered propeller would permit a certain number of revolutions, driving the sub under the

surface, before the drive shaft activated a mousetrap, which snapped shut on a soft rubber tube that served as valve, just as the mousetrap simultaneously spilled the small can of chemicals, which would produce a gas to purge the ballast tank, causing the sub to surface.

I doubted that he was really interested in my project, but he soon phoned me and then he came over with you, bringing his two sheets of drawings. We were in the submarine business! I was very young and could hardly believe that this man, who seemed made mostly of words, who uttered several thousand of them per visit (most of them over my eighth-grade head), could concern himself with my wild invention, as I fancied it to be. But he quickly let me know that he had won a university scholarship in physics and chemistry before he became a wordsmith. He told me how, in his youth in England, he'd dropped a large lump of metallic sodium off a bridge into a Birmingham canal near passing barges. Naturally, the sodium sputtered, exploded, flamed and smoked, drawing the attention of bargemen to it, and to himself.

Well, I experimented with Wystan's plans for some days, but none of his suggested paper-wrapped chemicals reacted to plan. But then, I wasn't a poet! I had no fragile paper on which poets write their songs—my paper wouldn't dissolve into song or power. But finally my sub housed a miniature engine, later a battery motor, and a radio-controlled rudder, which I made myself. Wystan's plans were never effectuated, but the sub survived as evidence of my engineering fantasies that continued into college. A few years ago I took that old model out of the attic for my son to boat in our swimming pool.

Brad wasn't the only Stevens child to receive Wystan's attention. Of Grace, the second eldest, Albert would say at times, "Grace is the living picture of her grandmother," and Grace would retort, "I wish I was only the picture of myself!" Angelyn discussed this problem with Wystan, who wrote for Grace's tenth birthday (March 5, 1942):

Happy Birthday
I'm sure the good fairy
Who watches your progress is glad
That you're more scientific than Mary
And more artistic than Brad.
May you never be nursed by a grievance,

May your mind approve of your face;
May the odds be in favor of Stevens,
And grace be given to Grace.

Wystan wrote these lines in the fly leaf of a book about
Matthias Grünewald, whose paintings he liked, especially one
of an angel with a cello-like instrument in hand, as Grace
often had; he gave the book to her. Angelyn helped Grace to
learn the cello and to perform at family musicals, such as the
one Wystan and I enjoyed in our first evening with the Stevenses. Angelyn asked Wystan, "Do you think Grace's interest
in music will endure?" And Wystan replied heartily, "Yes! If
it's properly encouraged." Wystan gave Grace and Angelyn
two tickets to a cello concert in Hill Auditorium, Grace's first
formal concert attendance; and now, years later, Grace and
her husband play music with their children, and Grace plays
her cello in local symphony and chamber groups.

In the spring of 1942, Wystan undertook to cure Angelyn
of her allergies, as she later wrote to me:

When I spoke to Wystan about feather allergy, he was
interested. I told him about my severe outbreaks of
rash and pimples caused by dust and feather particles,
but Wystan assured me that Kierkegaardian psychology would prevent my allergies.
In the attic of 8 Marshall Court I had a great bag
of goose feathers and down, brought by my mother
in steerage from Holland and given to me. My younger
sister was always after me for a share of the feathers,
but I refused, telling her I couldn't touch the feathers
due to my intense allergies. But when I told Wystan
these details he guessed at once that I was jealous of

my younger sister. In fact, I disliked her. Wystan *ordered* me to forgive my sister for any and all grievances, and to give her, *at once*, a share of the feathers. And to do it with conscious love in my heart. So I went up into the attic, I opened the big bag and stuffed two pillowcases with feathers for my sister.

I expected to break out in bumps and pimples, but not a bump appeared, not even a spot of rash. Wystan and his Kierkegaard cured my allergy, so that I'm fairly free of them to this day and have had some success in freeing my children of theirs.

This interested me because I had severe allergies to dust and pollen, just as my mother had; and taking Wystan's advice, as well as Angelyn's example, I consciously tried to purge my own ill will toward my mother and some of my brothers. I must have received some degree of Kierkegaardian fringe benefit, for today my old allergies are almost extinct, due not only to Wystan's healing powers but to regular intake of vitamin C. *Fides et medicina!*

As I became well acquainted with the Stevenses I was interested to learn that Wystan never discussed his homosexuality with his "truly Christian family," as he described them, but mentioned it to them just once with a characteristic, "By the way, I'm a homosexual man." They accepted his homosexuality along with his large humanity, for he had proven already that his sexual nature had nothing to do with the Stevenses, their children, or their way of life. But Christianity they did discuss, and often.

Angelyn, her face glowing, once dramatized for me Wystan teaching a Sunday school class:

He wore shirt, tie and jacket, which he rarely did, and the children sensed his intense nature, his presence. They followed his every word. In discussing Jesus's troubles and temptations he seized the chance to make the Devil real to those children. "Do you know what the Devil looks like?" He looked sternly at each of those young faces turned to him; "Hmmm? The Devil looks like me!" He gestured a hand before his face, unmasking the Devil as a real person like himself, like other persons they knew. Not one child failed to visualize the Devil as flesh and blood.

As Wystan got to know the Stevenses he said to me, "Now I know that a truly Christian home does in fact exist." His affection for the family grew, especially for Angelyn, to whom he entrusted poems in progress, memories, and dreams. When he autographed her copy of *The Ascent of F6*, he scrawled in black ink on the fly leaf: "The end of this play is all wrong because, as I now see, it required, and I refused it, a Christian solution." On the fly leaf of Angelyn's *Dance of Death* he wrote: "The communists never spotted that this was a nihilist leg-pull." On *The Orators* fly leaf he scribbled: "A catharsis of the author's personal fascism."

Angelyn showed me these books on a winter day in her sunny kitchen corner while she concluded: "These and other jottings Wystan made in my books and in his letters to me are proof of his conscious wish to grow."

Sometimes Wystan went to the Stevenses' bungalow and sat on the sofa, saying nothing, but apparently at peace as he soaked up family warmth. Angelyn recounted to me, "One evening Wystan came in after the children were in bed, Albert was studying and I was finishing kitchen chores. Wystan sat on the sofa thumbing a copy of *Life* magazine, then tossed it aside, saying, 'Now I've learned another American slang word —squirrelfood'!"

Once at Marshall Court, Wystan got some of us into his game of "Self-Images," challenging us to present our images as others might see us. The game proceeded with much hilarity as Wystan presented to Chester and us his own image as a gawky professor who talked above his students' heads while he paced "a moot stage of theory!" Chester volunteered a modest, demeaning word picture of himself, but was soon interrupted by Wystan: "Now, Christopher—were he here playing this game—would pull a picture from his mind's purse, slap it onto the table, then as quickly snatch it back, saying, 'No!

That's not quite right!' And fetch out another: 'Really, not this, either!' Then pull out others, but none satisfying, for dear Chris has an uncertain image of himself."

They finished the game, all of us laughing but none more heartily than Chester, who in those days had a clear image of himself as Christopher's successor to Wystan's love.

Wystan's affection for the Stevenses didn't end with his departure from Ann Arbor. In July 1942 he wrote from Caroline Newton's estate in Pennsylvania:

Dear Angelyn and Steve,
    I was to be inducted on July 1, but the Lord intervened at the last minute, making the authorities forget that I hadn't had a blood test for a year, and so put it off till August. As a result, I managed to finish the Oratorio on Saturday; I'll send you a typescript copy for comments. . . .
    How are you all? Is Brad making a fortune? Has Grace learned how to cook a roast? What new stories has Mary been writing? . . .

Much love.
Wystan

Later (August 1942) he wrote from 155 East Fifty-Second Street in New York:

Dear Angelyn,
    Thanks a lot for your letter. Chester gets back [to Ann Arbor] next Friday, I think, with instructions about how to deal with my books and records. I have bought myself another phonograph, because I want you and Steve to have the old one, as a very inadequate expression of gratitude for all your friendship and kindness.
    The weather here has at last turned cool enough to let one work properly, so I am having a lovely time writing and reading. Am reviewing the new Shaw biography by Hesketh Pearson, a pleasant excuse for writing an essay on Christianity $\times$ Bergsonism $= ?$

. . . I stayed with Blanchards' when I spent a week at Swarthmore two years ago, and liked them enormously. G. E. Moore is to be resident the second semester.

Love to all.
Wystan

P.S. Swarthmore sounds little "Pi." There is no bar.

On February 12, 1943, nine days before Wystan's birthday, Angelyn gave birth to a son, and the poet came from Swarthmore for the christening of his godchild, Wystan Auden Stevens. He brought with him a holograph manuscript of his "Mundus et Infans," ("for Albert and Angelyn Stevens"), and he attended the christening, as Angelyn recalls: "Our Presbyterian pastor combined elements of Episcopal and Presbyterian baptismal liturgy into one, enabling Auden to affirm his commitment to nurture the faith of Wystan Auden Stevens. The christening service was held within the chancel railing after regular Sunday services, and we all remember it to this day."

This Christian occasion was much to Wystan's liking, and he spoke proudly of it to me. Although Wystan stayed at Chester's apartment, he attended the christening alone, a private affair, out of Chester's world.

Three years later, in 1946, Albert "stood up" for Wystan in the old county courthouse on Huron Street, attesting to federal government officials that he had "known W. H. Auden for several years" and that the applicant was a good candidate for U.S. citizenship, which Auden was granted in May 1946.

Angelyn told me one time as we sat in the sunny kitchen of their home, now on Olivia Street (a few doors from the house where I and a group of students had baited a captive Auden in Professor Cowden's den on a frigid evening in 1940), how her children loved the bungalow in the garden at the end of Marshall Court: "Grace, especially, loved that bungalow and protested when we felt obliged to move to this larger house. When Grace was a teenager she went at times to baby-

[84]

sit in our former house on Marshall Court, and one night she came home with a thumb-sized piece of plaster she'd pried from a broken spot in the cellarway: 'Mom, you don't think I did wrong, do you?' I heard Grace, I understood why she wanted a relic from her childhood home, and I said, 'Grace, you didn't do wrong to take it.' "

Now when I think of Wystan in Ann Arbor, I think of the Stevenses and of Angelyn's exemplary concern for her children, a concern shared by Wystan from the moment he stepped into the children's enduring domain of First Home. In other towns and cities, Wystan recalled to me some of the good times at the Stevenses and especially our first sumptuously "common dinner" at Marshall Court in sun-gilded twilight when we said grace with "a common American family."

A common American family?

Ah, America—if only they were!

SIX

Time makes old formulas look strange,
Our properties and symbols change . . .
"New Year Letter"

FROM SEPTEMBER 1942 TO APRIL 1945 WYSTAN WAS TEACHING
at Swarthmore and "pegging away" at his new long poem,
The Sea and the Mirror. He went to Germany in April 1945,
a few days after his *Collected Poetry* was published, to serve as
an officer in the U.S. Strategic Bombing Survey, a mission of
which he spoke bitterly and briefly. By September 1945 Wystan
was in Manhattan, where I visited him; and I clearly recall the
feeling of relief we shared. History seemed to favor freedom;
peace influenced our philosophy.

In those days I served poetry's cause in my yeoman manner, giving occasional readings of Wystan's poetry with discussion periods, which ever prompted good audience response.
But I was soon to serve Wystan's image in a way I hadn't
imagined, via Robert Frost. In Ann Arbor, Wystan referred to
Frost as an "old meanie" and as "that old peacock," implying
that Frost had slighted or offended him in some way; but
Wystan praised some of Frost's poems, not only to me at the
breakfast table but in a 1930 essay on Frost's achievement.
However, it was near Easter 1946 when Frost displayed to me
his disfavor for Wystan Auden.

I was staying with Sidney Cox, my Cummington School teacher, at his home on East Wheelock Street in Hanover, New Hampshire. Frost stayed at the nearby Inn but spent many of his waking hours at Cox's house. Cox was a maverick Dartmouth professor of English, a gaunt, blunt, and clerical man with odd, ascetic warmth for his dispersed army of student followers; he was "old New England" personified and a long-time friend of Frost's.

In those years Frost slept most of the day so that he could fully enjoy nighttime hours. I came one evening into Cox's casually unkempt living room, where Frost sat on the sofa before the empty unlit hearth; he seemed huge to me, bulky and "hunky" (as Midwesterners say), a neat old man in a blue-gray worsted suit with a white shirt open at the collar, no tie. His large pale eyes dominated a broad and leathery face splotched with liver marks. Perhaps his face seemed broad because of his fairly small nose. The manner in which he moved and spoke, with sleepwalking deliberation, suggested that he was ill, which he wasn't, being at that time an active young septuagenarian. Frost perked up when the three of us began to talk. He had interest and curiosity in his eyes; he talked as easily as he breathed and soon proved that he was an able listener. He rambled from topic to topic and easily interrupted himself: "So you're from a Michigan farm? And you went to the University?" I asked him about 1223 Pontiac Trail and Frost explained: "Yes, I lived at that address when I was poet in residence. I was authorized to go ahead with my own writing and to radiate poetic atmosphere for the university. The house on Pontiac Trail was a handsome old Greek revival, and it was later moved to Greenfield Village near Detroit. Not because I lived in it but because it was an outstanding example of colonial architecture."

Cox was no admirer of our raffish Auden, or of Auden's poetry, but he soon turned the conversation that way because of my Auden connection. "No, I don't know anything about Auden's poetry," Frost claimed quietly. So I thought that was the end of Frost on Auden, but it wasn't.

That Easter week I made a dinner for Frost and Cox, for

Alice Cox was vacationing on a Carolina beach, and Wendell, the only Cox child living at home, was ski-camping in the White Mountains. During our informal meal, Cox announced that he had a writing seminar that evening, and would Frost care to attend? Frost said, "Well! Do they know I'm coming?" And Cox replied, "I told them that you might." I drove Frost and Cox to College Hall in the green Pontiac (which I had bought from Wystan on his departure from Ann Arbor), and I smiled to myself as I refrained from telling Frost that he was riding in Auden's old car. We paraded into a spacious lounge, where Frost regally assumed the prominent "throne" chair, even while he jested about a "padded chair of poetry" to Cox's assembled students.

As usual Frost was the platform master, relaxed before his young listeners and thoroughly enjoying his own words, which amounted to a monologue of free associations, an amiable stroll through his own mind. His vintage voice, pleasantly creaking at verbal corners, forestalled boredom in that the listener could never guess just what was coming next. Frost spoke of New England landscape, trees, national political figures, and a "pretty girl student who claimed she didn't believe in anything, and I told her that it wasn't possible to not believe in anything, that at least she seemed to believe in her own disbelief, and that she'd better believe that life was temporary, that sooner or later she'd graduate to death!"

The students chuckled with appreciation of his every word as he rambled on without uttering one word about books. Then with no warning Frost nodded at me, as I sat near him with Cox. "This young man is something of a poet and he's a friend of Auden, and I understand that Auden is subsidized by a wealthy lady . . ." I interrupted, casually, "Not so. Not subsidized! The lady, Caroline Newton, at one time paid for all his books and records. She gave him a second-hand car and a few other material things. But she told me she never gives him money. You know, he has worked mostly at teaching since he left Oxford, and now his books and lectures provide him a living." I said all this quietly, to a most attentive audience, but no one was more attentive than Robert ("Call me Robert"), who regarded me keenly—but without annoyance—for reasons I wasn't to know for years. Looking right at Robert, I went on: "Auden never made any secret of the gifts he got, and he's quite frank about his personal life. I know he doesn't mind my talking about this."

Robert nodded his gray head and said easily, without rancor or sarcasm, but with just a touch of humility, "Oh, I see. Thanks for setting us right." I cherished the "us." And he rambled on for hours more.

Later I learned that Robert's grandfather subsidized him as a young poet for many years, a fact that Robert kept from the world as long as he could.

Even while Robert talked, I realized that his freewheeling manner was related, if distantly and provincially, to Wystan's. In Robert's talk, even more than Wystan's, there was a gabby anarchy, a complete lack of allegiance to any single subject, a bantering tone which assured the listener that any given topic would not be run into the ground. It would be dropped and left, perhaps to be picked up again—the poet's prerogative.

On a night when Robert, Sidney, and I talked until dawn, Sidney mentioned that my "terrible farm novel" was autobiographical, so Robert soon got me to tell some of the brutal events leading to my father's suicide. Robert's interest was intense as he exclaimed, "Why, it's right out of Dostoyevsky!" Startled, I remembered Wystan using almost the same words on hearing the story.

Robert seemed eager to match my family tragedy, confessing the events leading to his son Carol's suicide in 1940. He told me about Carol's "nervous attacks" and how he'd hurried to Carol's side during a crisis, taking the train from Boston to arrive in Shaftsbury, Vermont, where Carol was working the small farm his father owned. There Robert had "talked day and night with Carol," trying to convince him "that he wasn't a failure," and that he should not "take up a pacifist attitude" in those war years. Carol had threatened various times to take his own life because he felt himself to be a failure as poet, farmer, and parent; but Robert's intervention at that point seemed successful: "He seemed to agree that he should go on living. He seemed to come around to my reasoning, so I went back to Boston. But I'd hardly gotten back there when I got a call that he'd shot himself," Robert finished with morose calm, bitterly summing it up: "So I learned how little influence a father has with his own son. What can a father do for such a son?" He dismissed the tragedy with a phrase I was to hear him repeat in later years: "Well, what does it all matter?"

It mattered to me, and I told Robert so: just a small matter of life and death. While we casually discussed my own pacifism, Robert regarded me with a wry, quirky little smile, but added no supportive word for pacifism. We talked of many things, especially outdoor and active life; and before the night was over Robert said, to my surprise, "You have strength and your own convictions. No one is going to meddle with your mind! Why couldn't I have a son like you?"

Robert returned to the subject of my family: "Charlie, you mustn't write about your family. It wouldn't be fair." But I retorted that I did write about my family and would continue to do so, in all fairness to truth, to human knowledge of human beings. In fairness to my father.

Robert cautioned: "Don't do it, Charlie. It's not the thing to do," he asserted quietly but dispassionately, leaving me to ponder his true feelings, his own family dilemma.

In later years, when I saw more of Robert in Vermont, he surprised me at times by asking, "What's new with your terrible brothers?" Nothing new, I told him, for indeed I'd seen little of them since I left home at the age of eighteen.

Certainly my first talks with Robert were all that an apprentice poet could wish from an old master, for Sidney had prepped me, Robert accepted me for what I was (no mean feat!), and each of us proved willing to talk on any subject. Perhaps because Wystan had listened to me by the hour, and perhaps because I was at home in almost any atmosphere and with almost any group of people, I was an able talker. Unlike almost any talk with Wystan, Robert and I didn't discuss sex that night, but we did later, with odd results.

Robert sat in the big wing chair facing the unlit hearth, saying early on, "I'll be the fire," and he was, a slow pale fire that could flame up on occasion. Sidney and I had a beer or so, with homemade cookies and coffee later, but Robert took not one drop of refreshment, nor did he leave the room for the nine hours of our "little talk," as he called it. None of us smoked. Almost no mention was made of books in general, or any book in particular, either those we'd read or those we hoped to write; and this was characteristic of Robert at that time in his long life. He told of his judo incident with Ezra Pound in England in 1914: "Ezra said, 'Give me your hand,' and I gave it, and soon I was flying over his head! Hurt? No." He laughed. "No, I wasn't hurt. I landed easily on the floor, as Ezra intended." But not one word was said about Pound's poetry.

When we talked about Ann Arbor, I asked Robert if his poem "Acquainted with the Night" was written about a tower clock in Ann Arbor, and he answered agreeably: "I'm often asked which tower belongs to that poem. But a poem is written about a feeling a poet has in him. It's true there was a clock on high in Ann Arbor, and I liked looking at it. And it's true that I wrote the poem in Ann Arbor. But the poem isn't about any one clock, or about Ann Arbor. It's about acquaintance with the night!" he ended, a bit puckishly.

The three of us were getting well acquainted with this night, as from time to time Robert pulled out a large silver pocket watch, held it away from him at arm's length to focus on it, squinted at it: "Well, well! Three o'clock already. The night's getting on." And pocketed the watch. Later, before our engaged, untiring eyes, he pulled out the watch again: "Well, well. Five o'clock. Getting near my bedtime." At last as chimes echoed from Dartmouth's Baker Library, Robert stood up and let out a leonine yawn. "Six o'clock already. People are getting up and going to work, so I'm going to bed."

I offered to drive him to the nearby Inn, but we decided instead to walk together to the edge of the green, within sight of the old Inn; and there Robert wanly said good night, giving us that twisted, quirky little smile as he turned to amble innward between heaped banks of frozen snow, a rotund overcoated poet, bareheaded in a wakening world.

The habit of prayer, by which I mean
the habit of listening.
Loren Eiseley, *The Star Thrower*, Introduction

After seeing Wystan only occasionally during the war years, I began to see him regularly in New York in 1946, and I attended some of his lectures in the New School, where capacity audiences attested to his American following. My companion was Amalia Larsen, who had studied with Wystan in Ann Arbor, where he had spoken fondly of her, describing her "with her mass of loose dark hair and large brown eyes" as "somewhat of a quotation from a Rossetti poem."

At a New School lecture on Shakespeare, Amalia and I sat down front, as we had in Angell Hall in Ann Arbor. We smiled knowingly when Wystan made conscious efforts to be "original" about Shakespeare's plays, and we weren't surprised when a few elderly academics got up and walked out in protest at Wystan's lack of humility before the Bard. Amalia opined that Wystan's teaching hadn't changed much since he lectured to us in Michigan.

Amalia and I were in love. I was divorced from my first wife after two years of a stormy Michigan marriage; Wystan had warned me against my first wife, but he liked Amalia not only for her poetic appearance but for her scholarly ability. When I came to Manhattan I stayed in Amalia's bohemian digs on Perry Street while she worked five and a half days a week for a utopian organization. From her apartment I walked the few blocks over to number 7 Cornelia Street to ring Wystan's doorbell. "Ya-as? Wh-oo is it?" he'd ask suspiciously over the intercom and then buzz me in. I'd trudge up the dark stairs to sit in the cluttered room on the one sofa-bed while he fixed tea and served it in grimy cups.

Wystan was as busy as he'd ever been, but not too busy to have tea and words with a friend; and he was curious about my rural life far from his "just city," so I told him in detail about the abandoned farmhouse I inhabited on a backroad in Fairfield County, Connecticut. It was a decaying salt-box cottage with no other habitation in sight; a brook that curled around the pasture slope was my only running water, and the outhouse at orchard edge had a generous half-moon window with a view. The large room I used in the farmhouse was timbered and graced with a great colonial fireplace; the dry-stone cellar held my "veges" and cider kegs, the woodshed my stacks of handcut fuel wood. An oak table by the kitchen window held my books and writing papers, a copper-smithed Rochester kerosene lamp shed light on my pauper's paradise. "Perhaps the best home I ever had," I told him.

Wystan chuckled over my "outhouse with a view" and went on to make basic comments: "So you pay no rent or utilities, you look healthy, hmmm, but aren't you lonely up there?" No, I told him, I wasn't lonely when Amalia visited me for a weekend or when I drove the green Pontiac down to Manhattan to "stock up on love and culture" as I expressed it to Wystan.

After questioning my squatterdom, Wystan took obvious pleasure in telling me about his cottage on Fire Island, a dune house that was as primitive as my abandoned farmhouse. "We pump the water by hand," he said, eagerly, making the motions, "like pumping water to your kitchen sink, as you described it, on your parents' farm in Michigan." Wystan had bought the cottage with James and Tania Stern, European friends, for a very small sum even by 1940s standards, and it was the only real estate he owned in America.

Despite his usual zest and nervous energy, I noticed that he appeared pale and tired, especially when he spoke briefly and with bitterness about his tour of duty with the U.S. Strategic Bombing Survey in Germany at war's end in 1945. He spoke cheerfully of Chester, who had worked mostly in New York City during the war. Chester had written to me often in the last war years, when he was in New York and I was in Michigan, but I never saw him at the Cornelia Street apartment.

One late December afternoon I parked the green Pontiac on Bleecker Street and walked past open booths, stalls, small shops, and pushcarts heaped with the world's foods; and as I stepped into Cornelia Street a wooden delivery wagon rumbled by, the horses' hooves clop-clopping in the short, narrow street. Huge snowflakes tumbled down, church bells tolled over snow-muffled traffic and as I passed Zampieri's Bakery, which exhaled hot, spicy Italian odors, I felt that (as Wystan himself asserted) "Cornelia Street was as good as in Europe." It was certainly exotic to me.

Wystan was at home, and I sat on the sofa among books, periodicals, the *Times* and the *News*, manuscripts, scrap paper, and nearly empty cigarette packages, which waited for Wystan to probe with an absent-minded finger, searching for that last fugitive fag. We traded gossip. Wystan was going to the Niebuhrs', I was in the city to take Amalia to Connecticut with me for a few days. Knowing Wystan's fondness for plum pudding (which he called suet pudding), I'd made a good one, aged it, and gave it to him, along with a bottle of my cider-champagne from the earth-floor cellar of my squatter's homestead. "Hmmm, you have all the riches," Wystan murmured.

As I sat talking with him, I was quite aware that my America was rewarding Wystan for his talent and industry; his books were widely read, his poems appeared in periodicals, he taught a few classes, he was in demand for lectures and readings, and he had no end of friends and invitations. Wystan was working on *The Age of Anxiety* but showed no more anxiety than he had before he became an American citizen and a national literary force. He was perhaps at the peak of his fulfillment as poet and person.

Wystan spoke fondly of his Village neighborhood. He agreed with me that Cornelia Street was too dark and narrow, yet he liked it for its old apartments, its family stores, and especially because the huge delivery horses slept almost under his apartment and traversed the street several times a day. He liked the Bleecker Street open markets and stalls; and there I went with him one winter afternoon. He stooped under sidewalk awnings of fishmongers and fresh produce dealers; he bought Zito's crisp bread and paused to examine a brace of brilliantly colored pheasants hung by the feet, their feathers ruffling in the cold breeze, waiting for Village gourmets to claim them.

In those days, veterans were seen everywhere and their roles were discussed, just as Wystan and I discussed our Nisei friend, John Nakamura, who was killed on the Anzio beachhead; John had been a student of Wystan's, a delightful presence at his at-homes, as well as a close friend of Amalia. For me, John was a tragic victim of war's injustice, and I confided to Wystan, "Good human beings ought to prevent their governments from promoting war. If each one of us as decent people would simply refuse to kill others, wars would wither away . . ." Wystan interrupted, bitterly: "War is as likely to wither away as the state is likely to wither away."

We had discussions of my quasi-vegetarianism and my pacifism, the combination of these serving as my quasi-religion; but Wystan had been brought up in an overtly Christian home, and despite his vigorous affair with Marxism in his twenties, he was a tribal Anglican, now a high Episcopalian, a Christian sojourner returned to his traditional faith. So I was surprised in the forties when some literati purported to be confused by the implications of his oratorio, *For the Time Being*, some commentators saying that "Auden is likely to become a Catholic convert." The forties were "a time of important conversions," including those of Robert Lowell, Clare Booth Luce, and Henry Ford II, but there was, in my opinion, little chance that our Yorkshire-Oxfordized poet would change ecclesiastical horses in midstream of his Protestant quest. As Angelyn Stevens, Ursula Niebuhr, and Anne Freemantle knew, Wystan's will to "vert" to Catholicism was a rumor, never a fact.

The one-room apartment on Cornelia Street had no proper kitchen, so Wystan ate in Village restaurants, and once he took me just around the corner on West Fourth Street to a lunch-counter cafe with a cheery flame on its front window grill. This place was "comfy" and inelegant; it served no liquor, beer, or wine; it had only a few small tables and booths; and it smelled of deep-fry oil, burnt toast, hamburger, chili, and coffee, with an overlay of soup-cauldron steam. We entered and stood looking for a seat in the busy eatery, and Wystan was "hmmm-ing" and "uh-uh-ing," making to leave, when a woman rose from a booth, took her coffee and sandwich to the one free seat at the counter, and waved us toward the booth. Wystan beamed and let out a voluble, "Th-thanks!" I did also. We squeezed into the narrow board seats, and Wystan, overwhelmed, half-rose to bow toward the woman and say with recital hall volume, "Uh, really, thank *you*!" The woman nodded gravely, bit into her sandwich as Wystan sank down into his seat, to rise immediately, adding, "Uh, very much!" then saying to me, "So *veddy* nice of her!" By now everyone in the place was aware that old-fashioned courtesy had resurfaced in rude Manhattan, and all patrons bent with renewed appetite to their noon repast.

Wystan ate as hungrily as he did every noon, after a morning of work, while he talked casually about any little thing in tones that carried to every ear. I don't recall just what we ate, but my scent memory remembers that our food tasted like the cafe smelled—Wystan's favorite fried America.

At teatime near Easter I arrived at Cornelia Street to find Wystan with a handsome woman he introduced as Rhoda Jaffe. Her resemblance to my Amalia was striking; I later described Rhoda to Amalia as "hefty and handsome, with brownish hair and a handy smile." Rhoda was at ease with Wystan, who spoke to her with familiar affection. She served us coffee from the kitchenette alcove and resumed her place on the cluttered sofa beside Wystan, where she continued penciling a clutch of typescript while Wystan and I talked in our rambling habit. Within a half-hour, Rhoda got up and gathered her things, preparing to leave. Picking up a holey brown cardigan of Wystan's and pouting like a housewife, she said, "Wystan, I'm going to mend this. It needs new buttons, too." Wystan: "Is it worth it, dear?" Rhoda: "Definitely, it is." She spoke in a feminine, teasing manner that would melt any male monument, and Wystan answered intimately, their tones and their eye embraces indicating to me that they were physical as well as intellectual lovers.

Wystan told me that Brad Stevens had left Ann Arbor and had showed up one day at 7 Cornelia. He didn't have his "ever unfinished" submarine model with him, but he had a great desire to find a career in the city, ultimately in design work, but for the time being he would work at anything to gain a livelihood.

As Brad wrote to me later:

Wystan gave me plenty of advice, and he gave me a part-time job building shelves in his apartment when he was away. What a mess, that apartment! He needed a large table, so he'd balanced a four-by-eight-foot plyboard on top of the small table and put rows of manuscripts, papers, mimeograph sheets, clippings, and books face down all over the plyboard surface. It seemed completely disorganized to me, but you know Wystan—he was making a book out of that mess. The place wasn't comfortable. Not for me, anyway. Wystan told me to help myself to drinks in the "fridge," but when I opened it I found only partly filled bottles of gin and vermouth, neither of which I needed in those days.

Naturally, I was at loose ends in New York. I was too young, too inexperienced and jobs were too hard to find. Furthermore, I couldn't fix myself onto anything that seemed suitable. So I soon returned to Ann Arbor, where I started off on various tangents that finally led to my career in design and invention. Had I stayed in New York near Wystan, he would have helped me find work I could live with, but I was glad enough to go "home" to Michigan, and I never regretted that I did. New York was not for me, much less Wystan's roost on Cornelia Street.

SEVEN

Spirit is willing to repeat
Without a qualm the same old talk,
But Flesh is homesick for our snug
Apartment in New York.
   "On The Circuit"

LIKE WYSTAN, I ADORED THE VILLAGE, THAT LOW-WALLED LOWER
Manhattan ghetto of intellect, creativity, and Old World
cultures. Generations and nationalities lived in its mazes of
streets lined with low buildings, unshadowed by the smog-
scrapers of Midtown. Here our heroes, martyrs, and bad guys
mixed in the democratic compost that made America. Here
Henry James and his opposite, Herman Melville, walked separate paths in Washington Square Park; and Abe Lincoln
(that lanky New World Napoleon of emancipation) walked by
Saint Mark's Place and crystalized his purpose in Cooper Union
meeting hall. Whitman, Emerson—even Thoreau—Edward
Hopper, and Eugene O'Neill knew and liked the Village,
where the pace is traditional. It is ever a temporary home of
the spirit for Italians, Slavs, Jews, Latins, and Orientals as well
as for those of us who cherish Old World ways; for despite the
New World "progress" of the encroaching city, Old World
vestiges of the Village continue to foster rich ethnic components
of our open society.

When I homed to nest in a sublet room or to shack up

on a spare bed or couch (or to cache myself in sleeping bag on a bohemian friend's floor), I was at home in the Village next best to my beloved New England villages; but second to none (during certain decades) were the coffee houses, chess bars, little theaters, lecture halls, galleries, bookstores, and cheap eateries. Most of my friends were Villagers.

From 1945 to 1953, Wystan lived in small apartments, such as the one-roomer at 155 East Fifty-Second Street, and later in the more sizable digs on Cornelia Street; but he spoke to me of needing a "homier nest," and finally in 1953 he wrote me from his newly leased Village flat on Saint Mark's Place: "Come around anytime."

The old russet bricks of 77 Saint Mark's Place were splashed with afternoon sunlight when I strode up the arched flight of stone steps above an English basement to find the Auden–Kallman button in the glassed entry hall, bringing Wystan out to his stairway landing to squint down at me before pressing the release buzzer. He was boyishly excited about his new home: "Come! I'll take you on a tour."

The large first (entry) room with high ceiling had a green marbled fireplace flanked by built-in bookshelves, which also incorporated Wystan's battered turntable with speaker equipment and his much-used collection of records and albums. A big shabby sofa and a swamped antique coffee table centered the cluttered room. I followed Wystan through an arch into a similar room at the front with another green marbled fireplace. This room was hardly furnished, except for built-in bookcases and Wystan's small work table just touched by sunlight from the generous nineteenth-century windows. To the right of this room, as we faced Saint Mark's Place, was a small room with its door to the stair hall nailed shut; the room had only a cot bed, on which Wystan slept, he said.

"Aren't the fireplaces handsome," Wystan enthused, and, yes, I thought of the previous century when those fireplaces heated the generous rooms. As we returned to the entry room, Wystan waved a hand at glass doors curtained and partly closed onto a deteriorating "sun room" with a soot-dusted vista of rusty fire escape ladders. The kitchen beside the entry had walls of thin white tiles, and Wystan placed a hand on them to praise their porcelain simplicity.

The gas stove, refrigerator, and kitchen sink with work space were gray-lighted by a big grimy window, the sill coated with some of the finest soot made in Manhattan. On the floor near the unclean stove was the big familiar supermarket brown bag crammed and bursting with garbage, topped with pungent coffee grounds, a half-pint cream carton oozing its last come-on to cholesterol, crowding a pert tail-end of Polish sausage. Wystan's staple tin of Bluebird orange juice, pinked open with beer-can opener, waited on the sink drain while the thirties refrigerator, with its topknot of coils, hummed a Gregorian-motored "Home Sweet Home."

The tour took only minutes, but Wystan sank into his overstuffed chair, sighing, fumbling for a cigarette and lighting it while he mumbled the history of the flat and his plans for redecorating it, painting "all of the interior with interesting colors." Facing us, to the left of the fireplace and above the bookcases, was a Blake watercolor (gift of Caroline Newton), casually framed, slightly askew. Blake posed as a beard-streaming God, kneeling on a cloud-raft, calibrating the planet below him with eighteenth-century calipers, but seeming quite at home in Wystan's "Soho-ish" hall.

I sat on the sofa beside a small but elegant Italian volume lying opened, face down; one of Wystan's holey socks waited patiently for a mate on the cat-hairy cushion near yesterday's *Times* folded open to a half-completed crossword puzzle. One of Wystan's three known neckties curled beside a sheaf of stapled manuscript, its typed pages curling in contentment, loved wherever it lay.

The coffee table bore its household harvest of books, periodicals, half-emptied coffee cups scummed over with cream, a dash of cigarette ashes for good measure, and a heel of French bread (too tough for Wystan's new dentures?). An oval platter served as ashtray, heaped with a homey Vesuvius of cigarette butts, ashes, bits of cellophane from discarded packs, a few martini-soaked olive pits, and a final cigarette stub issuing a frail plume of smoke from the top of the heap, signature of a dying volcano. This Auden-scape reeked of stale coffee grounds, tarry nicotine, and toe jam mixed with metro pollution and catshit, Wystanified tenement tang. Sighing contentedly above the spoor of his new place, Wystan puffed his "coffin pin," as I called it, and continued: "It's a sound old house, Charlie, solid as a rock. You like it? After I signed the lease, I met people in the Holiday Bar in the basement here who told me that Trotsky stayed in this house! That he wrote a book, or a pamphlet, which was printed in the basement!" Wystan's face was as lighted and happy as I'd ever seen it, but later I learned that the Trotsky connection was neighborhood legend rather than provable history, although Trotsky did visit and work in other houses on the street, and some of Trotsky's writings were printed on a small press in the basement of number 77.

From where I sat I could see Wystan's small table with his pale blue Olympia portable ringed with piles of paper, clipped sheaves of manuscript, and his cardboard student notebooks with black and white marbled design relieved with pen slashes where he had started a clogged nib; and I knew that the workbooks were full of pinch-penned words that scrawled toward the horizon, an ever-receding horizon of expression. Here he sat every morning in his un-cozy work chair, his back to the street, his head cocked to the papers beside the typewriter, his near-sighted bespectacled eyes peering at far-sighted literature. The generous Victorian windows afforded a glimpse of Saint Mark's Place crossing busy First Avenue, where ethnic shoppers milled along with American bohemians from one ethnic emporium to another.

Wystan asked me eagerly: "Did you notice the doctor's metal sign embedded in the brickwork by the entry? His offices were in this apartment. He was an, uh, economical abortionist." (Abortions were illegal then.) "Now and then some poor woman comes into the entry to press all the buzzer buttons until she gets me to the door to ask me to do an abortion! I tell her that I'm not the doctor, that I've just moved here, the doctor moved away, long ago, and I never met him, never knew where he went. But she doesn't believe me, she thinks I'm lying," Wystan said, looking at me sideways, and then sighing at the sympathetic red eye of his cigarette. "Girls come here sometimes, quite pregnant—such young things!—and ask for the doctor. Poor dears. I'm no use to them at all."

He was telling all this with true compassion, in a querulous, wondering tone—amazed that such things were happening to him in wide-open America!

Wystan adored the First Avenue open markets with sidewalk stalls and booths where capped and smocked street merchants hawked food in loud European accents: "Fresha feesh, chust in froma ocean," and "Looka da apples, lady, five pounds da dollah, lady." Foods were stacked as if to spill onto sidewalks from their bins, tables, boxes, and hampers in a profusion of plenty and in an ambience so earthy, vocal, and colorful as to make any air-conditioned supermarket seem like a cemetery of food. But Wystan warned me: "Now, Charlie, *some* of the food is fresh, but many of these stalls handle produce rejected by better markets. Just go to the best stalls and buy their, uh, best food, and you'll get the best bargains in the city."

At times I shopped there with Wystan, and once we stood in equinoctial sunlight to eat raw oysters as they were opened and handed to us one by one over a wet plank, the old Sicilian oysterman exchanging Italian quips with Wystan. In most cases, Wystan was a fussy shopper, fidgeting over purchases of vegetables, or shifting from one foot to the other in a little First Avenue bakery, unsure which flute of golden bread he really wanted, while other shoppers casually pointed at the loaves of their choice. But across the avenue, in Kurowycky's butcher shop, Wystan resolutely shuffled over the sawdusted floor to command his favorite sausages and chops. While lagging over his few purchases, he discussed food and local restaurants with me, as he always had, but concluded that "Eating at home is best of all!"

Auden's Saint Mark's Place was a kind of Manhattan home for me, or a second home in spirit, where I went for two decades, always certain to find the spark of friendship that was first kindled in a far-off college town. How many times I strode up those stairs, having phoned or written a postcard in advance, and always with the homey expectation of coffee and words, or a drink and words, sometimes a meal and words. But my innocent anticipation was slightly tinged with doubt, a low-key repulsion-attraction, the Square's slight dread of the overt queer.

After twelve years of Wystan-at-home, I was aware of our unvoiced and unformulated contest: Wystan was waiting for me to prove myself as person (if not poet) to him, and I was waiting to define him, to *name* him, to formulate his complex entity in my consciousness forever, as Friend, Brother, Poet-Mentor—I did not know then which, but hoped to know sometime. In later years I judged that we enjoyed the "force" of a friendship of opposites.

Fine, for me. But what was Wystan getting out of our calm, controlled, and nonsexual friendship? He was getting the best I had to offer: my offbeat, "amiable anarchist" wisdom, my ability (finally!) to laugh at life and to make Wystan laugh with me. Wystan the wordsmith loved words, and words were our purest staples. He never failed to inquire after the haphazard details of my life, which I gave him in outline: I lived in "functional poverty," as I called it, restricting my work life (and therefore my income) so as to pursue my hoped-for career as a writer. I lived nicely this side of mooching or welfare by doing part-time work for state agricultural agencies in Connecticut, graduating to part-time work for dairy farmers in Litchfield County. All very well, except that my writing failed to win publication, the big farm novel (a Hopwood Award winner) managed to remain unpublished, despite praise from editors and fellow writers. Frost had chided me in public: "Miller won all the awards and honors except publication"—which was witty if untruthful, for I had published in little magazines and in various collections.

Yet, as I told Wystan, my virtue of writing was my own reward. If I was humbled from the failure to publish, a failure shared by millions of yeoman writers (especially poets), it was nothing compared to the personal failure of my "great love" in the Connecticut countryside. Obliged to earn money, in hope of carrying off my scandalous young love (she was scandalously young for a New England community, and I "scandalously old" after one marriage and a good companionship with my Amalia), obliged or persuaded to get out and "make good," I'd moved to Vermont and converted my teenage hobby of stone masonry into a craftsman's career. I got a mason's union card and the freewheeling way of life that went with it, planning to work in leaf time and write in snow time. As I expressed it to Wystan: "I was a little miller-Melville, billy-budding it through the building trades, attentive to the Captain Veres of professional writing."

Within months of leaving Connecticut, I was a familiar figure on Vermont building sites, but sometimes I practiced my trade during winter months in Florida, Texas, California; a spate in Mexico, a good trip in Montreal. I wrote in rooming houses, in Sun Belt boardinghouses, in cheap hotels, and sometimes in the houses or barn studios of literary friends; a true "lonely" on the road, guiding the venerable green Pontiac through purgatorial traffic circles of urban hells in search of building sites at a time when America had plenty of them. But Wystan pointed out to me that the elusive American Dream, or my personal concept of it, waited beyond such building-site horizons.

I gave Wystan not only my dreams when I circled back like a homeless pigeon to his Village nest, but the comedy of my mobile life in America, and endless words about others' lives, for Wystan was ever fascinated with the lives of workaday "common Americans." It was my good fortune that he heard my unbeaten voice, frowned at my self-induced predicament, welcomed me in his unkempt flat, challenged my best and deepest feelings. And so helped to keep me alive and sane.

> *Could any tiger*
> *drink martinis, smoke cigars*
> *and last as we do?*
> "Symmetries and Asymmetries"

Wystan wasn't well. His gradual decline from fairly good health began after 1945, and by the late forties he had exchanged his remnant teeth for dentures. In the past, Wystan had suffered from occasional headaches, but now he suffered severe pain from an ailment that Dr. David Protetch described to me as "tuberculosis of the optic nerve," a mean disease for a reader and wordsmith. Dr. Protetch, whom we'd known from Ann Arbor days, told me, "It's a bad trip for Wystan, because the optic nerve can't be operated on, and drugs give only sporadic relief." So Wystan was obliged to take various drugs in order to work; then, as the dosages were decreased, Protetch prescribed barbiturates to ease Wystan off the drugs. But it was heavy going, and Wystan's face was puffed and creased almost beyond recognition, his eyes partly closed, his head drooping on his weary shoulders.

At this point, a photograph appeared on the front page of a New York review, and I can't forget my shock on seeing the brutal photo of ailing Wystan, or my annoyance when friends asked me, "What in hell is Wystan up to, now?" Nor was I about to forgive the editors who published such a photo. Over a period of months Wystan's condition improved and the puffiness decreased, but the wrinkles and cracks remained, a mud-flat map of Wystan's journey through pain.

My first full awareness of Wystan's deteriorated condition was in the mid-fifties, when he returned to New York from a long lecture tour. ("Charlie, no more tours!" But the tours continued, as surely as his health worsened.) He fairly groaned with fatigue. His lungs—his poet's bellows—squeaked in poor repair; and when he wheezed his way about the apartment, he shuffled rather than walked. He was a bit heavier, paunchier, flabbier, his face was pasty, and he squinted like a jack o'lantern when he lit a cigarette, the smoke (somewhat the color of his face) coiling around his head like an evil halo waiting to be sucked down into his sick lungs. Yet Wystan didn't complain. He was alert to complainers, quickly admonishing them, "No whining, now!" At times he would discuss "an interesting illness," like Kenneth Patchen's, in a clinical spirit; or he would mention offhandedly, "Sometimes I have these migraine headaches which just knock hell out of my work!"—not his temper or disposition, but his work—after which he always worked on, his dynamic mind driving his ailing body onward.

While Wystan sat before me on this particular day he was seized with a whole-body shudder, a head-to-foot spasm, ending with a huge "Buuuuuuuuooh!" And I recalled how he had given a big shudder at breakfast a few times, years ago in Ann Arbor, then exhaled in a huge baby "Boooooo," with loose blubbery lips to release the tensions of his wordsmith drudgery, after which he rose and went across the hall to his work table. Now, he actually had some of the horrors he had only rehearsed then. In earlier years it was a kind of yoga exercise, like a hawk preening and loosening his feathers; now, however, Wystan wheezed at the business edge of emphysema.

After this wheeze, Wystan smiled wanly at me, the tiny smile that signaled his survival of that moment, his face perking up as his breath dragged his dying cigarette coal to rosy life, saying once more, "Charlie, you don't know how I detest these tours!"

And I retorted, glowing with health and abeyance, "Well, Wystan! Why do you go on tours?"

"Aaah, for money! I have an annuity plan, you know, I pay a certain sum every month, so that when I'm sixty I'll retire, wealthy! Then I'll be able to do anything I desire. Travel. Loaf. No work!"

"And what good'll that be, if you lose your soul en route?"

"Hmmm?" Looking at me severely, he replied, "My dear, I *do* have responsibilities, you know."

I didn't know and I didn't ask just what his responsibilities were, but I knew that Wystan was wholly responsible to his art.

As we sat in the front room, Wystan stopped talking: "Listen!" A mouse was rattling paper bags in the kitchen, and Wystan peered toward the sound, a blissful little smile on his face. The mouse audibly rooted, rattled, and chewed a hole through thin walls of transformed forest. "Come out, come here, mousey! Co-oo-mme-on! Coo-oo-mme here, deah little mousey," Wystan cooed. But mousey kept to his lush trash bag, preferring to remain an invisible Stuart Little on Saint Mark's Place.

When Caroline Newton gave Wystan an original Blake watercolor in the late forties, it was an open New York anecdote that Wystan was a less than impeccable curator; friends came to his apartment to see it, telling me later that Wystan said, "Th' Blake? Aaah, ye-es," and went to the bookcase to riffle through piles of papers, poking, pawing here and there, until at last, "Aaah, *here* it is!" handing over the irreplaceable work of art, which was little longer than a sheet of typing paper, if thicker and generations older. Its faint purples, its cloud on which a Blake-featured God knelt to put his very real calipers down to measure Earth (and consequently look not a little bit baffled): this work of art would grace any creative room, but I thought it looked completely at home as it hung, slightly askew, on Wystan's wall above his bachelor anarchy of books and papers.

"Wystan! Aren't you afraid the Blake will be burgled?" I wondered.

"Not aa-tall! Whenever we are burgled, they take a radio, electric clock, the record player. If we had a telly, they'd take it. What *would* a pawn shop or fence do with an original Blake? It's quite safe with *our* kind of burglars!"

In the early forties Wystan was a notably light drinker, enjoying a glass of wine at dinner, and on rare occasions at lunch, but hardly touching hard liquor. By the late forties, he was a regular metropolitan drinker who gradually became a heavy drinker, mostly of good wines. I noticed at Saint Mark's Place that his first drink of the day was usually at one P.M. with his luncheon, a glass of wine or beer, never enough to interfere with his steady production of prose and poetry or his public appearances. One of Wystan's admirers recently told me that he'd seen Wystan stand by the kitchen clock, waiting for his agreed moment of liberty, one P.M. on the dot, time for the first drink of the day; yet I doubted the full truth of the story—it sounded to me like one of Wystan's charades of the moment rather than a habit; for if Wystan really wanted a drink at any hour, he'd take it and to hell with the clock.

Wystan and I discussed Dylan Thomas, a hearty drinker at the time of his successful reading tours in America and in the heyday of *Under Milkwood*. But shortly after Dylan's alcoholic death, I came to Wystan's apartment, depressed with the tragedy. Wystan was grave but natural, saying, "I saw Dylan on Twenty-Third Street, near the Chelsea Hotel, just days before the end. He was carrying a big bag of groceries and bottles. He was, uh, helplessly sober!" Wystan said this quietly, obviously moved by Dylan's sudden departure. It was tea time in the lonely flat, and Wystan commented pensively on Dylan's sporadic drinking problems but concluded in his old puckish manner, "Let's just have a *little* drink—shall we?" And so we did.

When I started working part time for Encyclopedia Britannica in New England, I suggested to Wystan that he add a new set of the Britannica to his library.

"Hmmm, not a new one. But I'd like an eleventh edition, if you can get one for me."

Many literary people place high value on the landmark eleventh edition, but I told Wystan, "This 1953 edition retains the best of the traditional articles found in the eleventh, including those by Saintsbury. And the new edition is updated with world information."

"Now, Charlie! I have all the world information I need.

If you can get me an eleventh, I'll be obliged to you," he said in that tone which precluded debate.

On my next trip from New England I went up the stairs with the first armful of the thirteenth edition, which, I assured Wystan, had most of the eleventh in it. I couldn't get hold of an eleventh edition, though I'd tried. Wystan gladly seized the offering of pale green volumes and I trotted down for others, he meeting me on the stairway until we "hustled" them all in and piled them on the cluttered floor at the end of the sofa, Wystan glancing at them with acquisitive curiosity.

As we sat down to coffee, I was braced to hear Wystan say, as millions of knowledge-hungry Americans did, "I've always wanted to own a Britannica!" But he refrained from saying it while we sat over coffee, speaking casually about "the rewards of reference books." He scribbled a check for fifty dollars ("Very reasonable, Charlie"); Blake's caliper-ing God looked over our heads, and the thirteenth edition dozed quite at home near empty wine bottles, the cats' bowls, old newspapers, and various visiting books in the apartment where it would rest for two decades.

Although Wystan declined to discuss with anyone the number of copies of his books sold around the world, he eagerly discussed how and why they were or weren't sold, his pet peeve being any publisher who failed to keep his books in print and available to book lovers. At mid-century most new books were sold in local bookstores, whereas now most are sold through book clubs and corporate-chain bookstores; Wystan appreciated these personal bookstores, and I'd been in several with him when he made a beeline for the poetry shelves—or, alas, poetry shelf—often the meanest section in the store, to see what poetry titles (not excluding Auden titles) were offered. At such times Wystan said nothing to the bookseller, but he did want to check up on him; and in his travels he went to the best bookstores in the same spirit a gourmet goes to renowned restaurants, to check out their taste.

Wystan and I often talked about books, but he preferred to talk about raw life: our likes and dislikes, adventures, and dreams were aired in haphazard fashion. Food, far more often than drink, was a favored topic, and Wystan's kitchen often seemed to be as much the heart as the belly of his house. When Wystan mentioned the past, it was often in terms of food, of holiday meals and the persons who prepared them. This "food worship" seems to be peculiar to persons reared in homes where the kitchen is the center; and the affection is especially strong when Mother prepares favorite foods for Child, as did Wystan's mother and her cook.

When we talked about food, Wystan sometimes asked me questions about the farm kitchen of my Michigan childhood, where an old Glenwood range was warm year-round and ever adorned with cooking pots, pans, and kettles from which our farm-grown foods emerged in nutritious rotation throughout the seasons. Once we discussed the implications of the farm kitchen where we ate most of our meals, where I bathed in a galvanized tin tub, where my older sisters washed my hair, where my parents whipped and "strapped" me, where I learned my brothers' and sisters' sex as they washed or bathed. (My parents, however, succeeded in never being seen by me as they bathed.) Later, in Latin America and in parts of Europe, I came to know one-room houses sheltering nine or more children with their parents in a compost of food–shelter–sex, a forcing bed for their future behavior.

Chester took no part in these discussions; in fact, he was usually absent from the flat. But I recall a time when he took me into the kitchen to point out his clam pots and related, with garrulous pride: "When the Stravinskys came to dinner, I steamed dozens of clams and we had oodles of broth to slurp," and so forth. I stood listening, my feet fastened to the gummy floor, wondering if I should give the ménage an exotic treat: scrub the kitchen floor! But Wystan and Chester loved their kitchen, not for any clinical cleanliness, but as a mouth-alimentary-canal-altar.

Wystan shuffled in carpet slippers from the kitchen with yet another cup of creamed, sugared coffee in hand and a strained smile on his striated face while Chester stood by the stereo set raving about a crabmeat mousse he'd made. Wystan gave me a slight wink, reminding me that he shared my preference for good plain food rather than concoctions of palate-crazed chefs, and he sank with a wheezy sigh into his big chair near the sofa and cluttered cocktail table, his work table a decent distance away; he took up the folded newspaper, half-smiling at a nearly finished crossword puzzle, as if he'd penciled onto tiny blank squares H-O-M-E.

> *Thou shalt not do as the dean pleases,*
> *Thou shalt not write thy doctor's thesis*
> *On education,*
> *Thou shalt not worship projects nor*
> *Shalt thou or thine bow down before*
> *Administration.*
> "Under Which Lyre"

In January 1954 Wystan was to give the Abernathy Lecture at Middlebury College. I lived nearby, and knowing that he happened to be staying at Norman Holmes Pearson's place near Yale, I phoned, offering to meet his train in Burlington or Montpelier; or, I could drive down and fetch him to Middlebury. But he said, "Noo-oo, my dear, that won't be necessary . . . see you there on Tuesday, at President Stratton's house."

Although I was regarded as "a local character," a "recluse of Ripton," and a social nonentity, the Strattons knew about me through Robert Frost, so I phoned Mrs. Samuel Stratton to tell her that I'd call for Wystan on the afternoon of the twelfth. She graciously inquired about the little solar house I'd built with my own hands on the mountain and said she hoped to see it sometime. Her tone and words made me look forward to my first visit at the president's house.

The snow was high, the temperature low, much as it had been in Ann Arbor, just fourteen years earlier to the week that I'd first met Wystan on a memorable weekend. I arrived at Stratton's house at two P.M., and Wystan came to the entry hall carrying his venerable brown tweed overcoat, moving past the matronly Mrs. Stratton, who was giving me a friendly word. Wystan swung the front door open. "Come on, Charlie, let's go downtown and get something to *eat!*" Mrs. Stratton clung to her composure, looking steadily at me as she stood in the wide doorway in pale northern sunlight; Wystan flapped into his overcoat and stumbled down the snowy walk, saying clearly and crankily, "I'm starved! You know what she gave me for luncheon? A dab of cottage cheese! And finger sandwiches on Wonder bread! Not even a drink!"

As we walked away I turned my head slightly to see Mrs. Stratton standing in the doorway, a Middlebury matron watching rude children leave her house. Wystan was, of course, bare-headed in the near-zero air and wore neither gloves nor scarf; however, we were soon seated in Lockwood's Restaurant, where Wystan devoured a roast ham meal in a matter of minutes, three Vermont loggers watching him doggedly as he outwolfed them.

Wystan seemed fairly well recovered as he recited, for the benefit of the quiet restaurant, "Imagine, finger sandwiches on gooey white bread. And weak coffee—on a day like this, after traveling through three states to get here!" He leaned back, sighing as he lit up his cigarette and nursed his mug of coffee. Yes, he told me, he was tired, but not too tired to continue drubbing the president's house: "My lecture tonight shan't be as *stingy* as the luncheon they gave me!"

Wystan talked about Chester, omitting everything but Chester's latest achievement in poetry; and he discussed his pleasing residence as a research professor at Smith College. At length I said, "Wystan, I want to drive you up to my cottage on the mountain in Ripton. It'll be about an hour, round trip." But no—"Can't afford the time, Charlie. I must get back to the house and get some work done."

At another time Wystan had stayed in Ripton, at the Bread Loaf School of English, when I was out of the state; he had spent an evening at Robert Frost's Homer Noble Farm, where the cook, Ma Jencks, a doughty Englishwoman, had spoken against "Mr. Auden, who deserted his England during the War;" but Wystan (as several persons of the household recounted to me) charmed Ma Jencks, helped her wash dinner dishes, and "won her over" as one more Englishman who "settled in the United States," as the Pilgrims from Plymouth, England, had done!

Wystan and I went along the snow-covered green to Dike Blair's Vermont Book Shop, where he was mildly pleased to find some of his titles in stock. As he autographed them for Dike, he said to me so that Dike could hear it, "Really, he doesn't have enough poetry here!"

That night, subzero wind swirled out of Vermont skies, but a thousand or so respectful collegians heard Wystan talk (as my journal noted) about

> the Verbal Society and Community of Belief; a poet writes poems for the fun of it, and hopes the reader will have fun, too. Wystan didn't repeat his old precept, "A poet is a revolutionist who wants to convert his reader to a verbal society," for Wystan has little revolution in him now. He is a traveled poet who can expect few surprises in people, and can only hope to continue making his own poetic surprises.

Wystan's lecture part of the program was less than lucid, and his own preoccupied delivery was further complicated by a faulty sound system; but his reading of new poems—"Mountains," "Woods," "Lakes," "Islands," "Plains," and "Streams" —was better. My journal continues:

> W's reading is blasé compared to that of the passionate young Englishman of fourteen years ago who read his Yeats and Freud poems to our Poetry Club in Ann Arbor when those poems were new. Then, his voice was rich with conviction. Then, he nearly cried. Now, he nearly yawns.

The reception at the Strattons was the usual, with coffee, cakes, punch, and too many people shunning the paradoxical poet (just as the crowd did at Dylan Thomas's reception at the nearby university months before, prompting Dylan to say to me, "These people aren't interested in talking to me, so let us get the hell out of here!"—which we did). Here, however, a few eager students waited to question Wystan; and I saw a tall, intense student reporter pose his clipboard at Wystan's lapel and scribble the poet's dictums, one of which was, "Senator Joe McCarthy? He'll take care of himself if given enough rope!"

The students soon left, for it was late, and Wystan turned with relief to the spacious living room with its cocktail table, the very sight of which made him talkative. He was coolly polite to Mrs. Stratton (President Stratton himself was out of town); the college chaplain, Professors Brown and Munson, and I were able to enjoy Wystan's postlecture levity. The young college chaplain asked about ecclesiastical Rome, but Wystan turned the conversation to the American representative to the Vatican, Clare Booth Luce: "You know, of course, that 'luce' means 'light' and that lights often go out in Italy? And citizens shout for the light to be turned on again? Well, everyone in Italy knows that every night Madame Luce dreams that *some day* she may appear on a Vatican balcony while the multitudes below chant, 'Lu-chay! Lu-chay! Lu-chay!' " The chaplain wriggled in glee, Mrs. Stratton smiled with tight lips but produced a fifth of bonded whiskey, placing it near Wystan's elbow on the cocktail table, where he had stationed himself near the glasses and ice cubes. Wystan seized the bottle, raised it to squint at the label, and then poured himself a large glass nearly full; he couldn't wait until the rest of us had served ourselves more modestly. Taking a healthy gulp, Wystan blinked at me, emitting a hearty, "Aaaah! That first taste." We all chortled sympathetically, but Mrs. Stratton looked reprovingly at him.

As the liquor-released talk got into high gear, Wystan took another half-glass of whiskey and Mrs. Stratton rose from her chair, took the bottle, looked at it closely as if to memorize the Plimsoll line, and carried it to the cabinet, clunking the door shut on it, while we all pretended not to see and talked on. William Blake, college English departments, President Eisenhower, and the Hillary–Hunt triumph on Mount Everest got a good going over; and when Everest was mentioned

Wystan gave me a fixed glance, which must have meant, "What about *The Ascent of F6?*" But I didn't ascend to his idea, and the conversation slogged on. Wystan asided to me, "Imagine what I got for *dinner*! *One* lousy little meatball, with a *spoonful* of spaghetti, like that . . ." I was ready for another trip to Lockwood's Restaurant, but Wystan supped on whiskey as best he could.

Near midnight, Wystan ducked his head, wiped his face with his hands, gave a great shiver of fatigue, and fairly groaned, "Ooooh, I, uh, *caaahn't!*" We all sprang to our feet, apologies were mumbled, but suddenly Wystan was relaxed and genial as he followed us to the entry hall, joking about Middlebury's "igloo weather," and chanting, "Now, in the Bahamas / They wear only pajamas!" To me he said, "See you later, in New York."

As I stumbled out into the subzero Vermont night, I marveled that Wystan's day had begun at six or seven A.M., and proceeded with nearly two hundred miles of roundabout train travel (a British-style "ramble" on our Boston and Maine railway), unpredictable food, a major circuit lecture, countless new faces and voices, and a few thousand unprogrammed words passing through his mind and dentures: he might well be weary. I turned to see him smiling at us, standing back from the presidential portal as Mrs. Stratton swung it shut: a provincial Parnassus closing shop at the stroke of twelve.

Since Merit but a dunghill is,
I mount the rostrum unafraid:
Indeed, 'twere damnable to ask
If I am overpaid.
　　　"On The Circuit"

During the fifties I attended some of Wystan's readings, none of which were showman affairs in the manner of Robert Frost or Dylan Thomas. When Frost gave an Abernathy Lecture in the fifties, the Middlebury College auditorium was packed to the rafters, with standees on three sides; laughter, cheers, and broad smiles abounded, for Frost the showman wanted to connect with collegiate audiences in the spirit of his line, "The way to wisdom is partly mirth." In this spirit, however, Frost's readings were often an escape, just as Wystan's were intellectual exercises in a long age of anxiety.

From the fifties on, a chronically exhausted Wystan often repeated to me that he was "through with tours," but he continued to endure them; and he mentioned his plan "to write a great verse drama" because, "you know, Goethe wrote the last parts of *Faust* when he was in his eighties." And Wystan expected to live to be "uhmmm, eighty-seven," a goal which his writing and "living dangerously" precluded.

There were light moments during Wystan's readings, and I observed one of them at the University of Vermont in the fifties, when he was introduced by a callow student chairman of the lecture series: "We are pleased to have with us tonight the well-known poet, William H. Auden." In the tittering applause that followed, the chairman resumed his seat on the platform. Wystan leaned toward him to ask quietly, "What school are you in, here at the university?" The chairman replied: "School? Oh, agriculture." Wystan said: "Aaah, I see!" And he went to the rostrum to deliver one more serious lecture-reading, which was well received by those who prized poetry and ideas.

One afternoon on a visit to 77 Saint Mark's Place, I was sitting and talking over coffee with Wystan and Chester when I became aware that Wystan was glancing at his wristwatch every minute. I got up as if to leave, but Chester said, "Sit down, please, I'm talking to you." In a few minutes Wystan rose from his chair, picked up his battered leatherette letter-case, grabbed his brown tweed overcoat (minus several buttons), mumbled a "See you later," and went out the door. "Wystan has a reading in Brooklyn," Chester said matter-of-factly, and he continued his metropolitan gossip while I thought about Wystan's complete lack of self-consciousness in his person or appearance. Had he looked into the mirror, he would have seen his old striped tie quite twisted under his collar and a lock of unwashed hair sticking out like a horn behind his left ear. Were his pants zipped up? He wouldn't know unless he happened to look or feel. Were his socks matched? Well, *once* they were—when he'd bought them, or received them as a gift. What did such details matter to Wystan?

Several times Wystan mentioned to me his master plan for readings and lectures: he accepted almost any paying appearance but generally refused to appear in the same place twice, for he believed, perhaps correctly, that he gained new readers with each public appearance, and so he meant to spread his appearances across a seemingly inexhaustible American stage. But he relaxed his no-repeat rule for certain places, including Yale—where he had collegial ties with Norman Holmes Pearson—and Harvard, which he admired from a distance. He did, however, refuse return appearances at the University of Michigan, writing Professor Bredvold, "This does not mean that I have forgotten my first love: like Dowson I shall say, 'I have been faithful to thee, Ann Arbor, in my own fashion,' and maybe . . . I shall be able to come back. . . . I hope so." But he didn't.

The New York YMHA poetry series platform featured Wystan several times when scheduled by John Malcolm Brinnin, the program director, who made its readings eventful; Wystan's were serious, none soaring. Manhattan friends often gave me their impressions of an Auden reading or appearance, as one quiet critic did:

> I went up to Fordham University to hear your friend Auden read to about two dozen rather cowed students, most of them women. Charlie, Auden was like a character from outer space. Or should I say that he was an absent-seeming poet reading his poems aloud to himself. We tried but we failed to relate to him as a person.

Happily, however, good critics and careful readers continued to relate to Wystan's published poems, and that was what he wanted.

Wystan talked seriously to me of my "delayed career" in writing and suggested that I travel in order to escape my "punishing America" during that oppressive McCarthy period of political witch hunts and Eisenhower complacency. I spoke of going to Mexico and all of South America in time, so Wystan gave me a copy of Isherwood's *The Condor and the Cows*, a Latin American travel book, which I read avidly, soon returning it.

"Well, how did you find it?" Wystan asked, eagerly.

"It made me decide not to go where Christopher went."

Wystan threw back his head and rocked with a belly laugh. "Ohohohohoho! I must tell Christopher."

Several times, up to 1957, Wystan offered me the use of his villa on the Neapolitan island of Ischia. One afternoon we sat in the front room of his flat, Wystan fixing me with his weary eyes: "Now, Charlie, you know you're welcome to stay at Ischia during the winter months, where you could write, undisturbed. You need the change! You'd not have to pay rent and you could get some fruit and veges from the garden. Food is ridiculously cheap there, but you mustn't use much water, as it's dear. You'd bathe in the ocean. You'd get by on very little money and you'd get a lot of writing done, I'm sure." He looked at me keenly, squinting behind the tiny genie-plume of cigarette smoke curling toward his tired eyes. "Hmmm?"

"No, but thanks." I was resolved not to go to Italy, for I had neither the funds for passage nor the luxury of time away from my sporadic masonry work that brought me enough money each month to keep me "caught up to two months behind" in my Vermont mortgage payments, as I explained to Wystan.

And so I remained in America, not underpaid for my "amiably anarchic" way of life, as Wystan described it.

1223 Pontiac Trail, Ann Arbor. Auden's first leased "house with garden and garage" in America. This studio house rests on the cellar foundation of a colonial house once occupied by Robert Frost. Wystan A. Stevens

Kitchen, 1223 Pontiac Trail, with entry hallway and living room in the background. Wystan A. Stevens

Auden with Ann Arbor friends: front row, Mrs. Esther Rettger and Mary Stevens; back row, Grace and Angelyn Stevens, Auden, and Prof. James Rettger. Albert K. Stevens

Auden at the railroad station, Ann Arbor, 1942, with Chester Kallman. Auden has his habitual carton of cigarettes in hand. Albert K. Stevens

1504 Brooklyn Street, Ann Arbor, where Auden lived with Chester Kallman and Strowan Robertson in 1942. The house was leased from Thomas A. Knott, and Auden wrote to friends, "It's a divinely Victorian house." Wystan A. Stevens

Albert and Angelyn Stevens on vacation, Niagara Falls, 1942.

*Charles Miller, spring
1946.*

Chester Kallman in the 1940s. Edward Kallman

77 St. Mark's Place, New York City, where Auden lived from 1953 to 1972, his longest place of residence. John Button

77 St. Mark's Place entrance; Auden's flat was one flight up. He was pleased that Trotsky had once visited the building and utilized the Russian printing press in the basement. John Button

Wystan Auden in the early 1940s, when he had completed For the Time Being *and* "The Sea and the Mirror," *but before his wartime tour of duty in Germany, a journey that marked him physically and psychologically.* New York Times

Wystan Auden at the door of his "grace and favor" cottage in Oxford, months before his death. New York Times

EIGHT

How should we like it were stars to burn
With a passion for us we could not return?
If equal affection cannot be,
Let the more loving one be me.
"The More Loving One"

IN EARLY 1959 I SUBLEASED AN ENGLISH BASEMENT APARTMENT
in Saint Mark's Church garden apartments and began to see
my neighbor Wystan almost daily, becoming involved in his
personal life somewhat as I had been in Ann Arbor.

When I phoned Wystan one evening to add something
to our recent discussion of Gogol and Nabokov, he answered
excitedly: "Charlie, come on over here, right now! I've got a
case of champagne left over from a party, and you *must* help
me drink it." I strode the few blocks in minutes, and we
commenced a bubbly evening, Wystan slumped in his big
chair near the entry, no music throbbing the smokey air as the
cork popped from the first bottle. Wystan poured a large glass
for himself, a small one for me; and this I resented, until I was
glowing and acknowledging that a little bit of the bubbly
went a long way with my country constitution.

Wystan orated on the current Land Bank scandal: "Imagine it! Farmers being paid for *not* raising crops. None of us
would think of complaining until the government wrote a
check for one million dollars to pay a Western farmer for *not*
growing his usual crop. It had to come, sooner or later, to a

million-dollar payoff, for this is America!—where the whole system of negative patronage is a bit loony."

I interrupted: "Our government buys not 'dead souls,' but 'dead acres'!"

"Precisely," Wystan agreed, sipping deeply at his very live champagne. "The basic concept is wrong. The government must find a way to make use of our surplus crops, since half the world is hungry. Really, it's immoral to pay—to bribe!—farmers for *not* growing food. It would be better if farmers were *required* to raise certain crops that are needed nationally. For instance, the government should help our farmers to develop, uh, olives. And grapes. Things we tend to import rather than produce." Wystan was in spirited form and concluded that he was ready to accept "even a *half-million* for *not* writing the longest verse play in the language!"

Next, he gave the national postal service a good going over: "You know, Charlie, that consumer groups tested our mail deliveries and were able to prove, by the postmarks, that a letter mailed from Chicago or Seattle arrived in downtown Manhattan sooner—sometimes *days* sooner—than a letter mailed from uptown. A letter addressed to Saint Mark's Place may take a day from Chicago, but five days from 110th Street! It just doesn't make sense."

By the time we got the U.S. Post Office on a practical and profitable course, Wystan had uncorked the third bottle and fairly bubbled with statistics, sociological arguments, and governmental reform. He had drunk at least twice as much of the good New York State stuff as I had, but I doubt that he felt any better than I did.

Popping open a bottle, holding it at a forty-five-degree angle, Wystan kept talking, not noticing that the sweet foam was pouring down his pants leg, while he said in convivial zest, "Don't you just *love* o-o-old bubbly?" And I answered from on high, "I've never had much . . ." He quickly gestured with the drooling bottle. "Here! Do have some more!"

Pulling the bottle back to safety, he filled his own tumbler full, leaning to slurp the foam, blindly holding the bottle out to me. Blake looked over our whirling heads at safer subjects; the long, thin, expensive cat leapt from floor to stereo shelf to top bookshelf, and Wystan's cigarette snuggled onto a bed of butts and ashes, indulging the rare luxury of going out. I dimly remember thinking that we'd got the "United States stated" when, sighing deeply, or adjusting his wheeze, Wystan looked at me steadily and began the Main Speech (while I stared, a bit numbly, at his lined, anxious, and now sweating face, which seemed, as it were, to echo, "just *love* o-o-old bubbly," the vowels bubbling from his moist lips).

Wystan was saying: "In America, everyone wants to be loved, but almost no one wants to love. In Europe, one makes a conscious choice, whether to love or be loved. A personal consciousness of the impending choice is a good thing. But in America there's no choice, no consideration—nothing more than keening and craving for love. Every son and daughter of matriarchal America cries for love, instead of giving it. Perhaps, more than anything else, this is what is wrong with America."

Later, I tried to seed the best of that evening in my journal while my mind mulled over it in lonely bachelor hours above my own work table. Wystan had gotten to the heart of the "lonelies" dilemma, but I pondered on the reasons why Wystan himself was a "lonely" in America. Naturally, after his eighteen years coupled with Chester, Wystan had "married" problems; Chester had long since declared his sexual independence and was often away, usually involved with other men, while Wystan was usually alone. Too much alone. If one hadn't experienced it many times, one would hardly believe that Wystan's listed telephone didn't ring for hours on end, or for days; for he belonged to no group, no club, no faculty (for most of his Manhattan years), no company, or corporation. He was, truly, "One after whom none think it worth to turn."

Yet, I liked to think that Wystan's loneliness wasn't the only reason for our long talks, for I, too, was something of a "lonely," having no use whatsoever for the neon jungle of bowling alleys, roaring bars, race tracks, clubs, card parties, or movie houses. Wystan enjoyed no sports, not even walking.

It was unfortunate that Wystan, like many intense creators, was isolated from regular family participation. The Stevenses and Niebuhrs gave him some comfort, at times, but neither of these families was in the city. Elizabeth Mayer continued to be his great friend, but she was not the matriarch of a numerous family. And even though Wystan had innumerable acquaintances and a few warm friends, he remained, in the eyes of society, an oddball bachelor who lived behind walls of books in the raucous East Village, a lonely eminence of his Third Sex minority. His peers were, like himself, cosmopolitan internationals, brilliant and creative figures—Eliot, MacNiece, Stravinsky, Lincoln Kirstein, Forster—whom he met for brief visits before he returned to his lonely labors. Occupation: writer. Occupational hazard: loneliness. And relative isolation.

By January 1959, Wystan's life was beginning a darker phase than any of us recognized, since he disliked complaining and ever refrained from discussing his one-sided passion for Chester. But Wystan was happy with the advent of Emma and Josef Eiermann in his new summer home at Kirchstetten, Austria. "They came with the house," Wystan told me, chuckling. "They are brother and sister, very earthy old creatures. They are to have a part of the house for the duration of their lives. And they let us live in the other parts of the house," he quipped. Over the years I heard many stories of the Auden–Eiermann master–servant relationship. While Wystan loved and respected the Eiermanns, he added his own puckish appreciation: "Charlie, they are the earthiest creatures imaginable, and Chester knew at once that they are sibling lovers! They have lived together since childhood, they survived war and expatriation, they are so inseparable that they sleep together!" Wystan looked keenly at me, chuckling; so I wasn't surprised when I later read in his "Elegy" (to Emma Eiermann), ". . . siblings can live in a bond / as close as wedlock." Wystan concluded, "They team up and run the house and garden nicely. We're lucky to have them."

However lucky Wystan was to have the gnomic Eiermanns as caretakers, it was his characteristic "luck" not to have a more normal couple with children to grace his house and garden, if only at certain hours, on certain days.

While one of my missions was to make Wystan laugh, it wasn't as easy as it had been in our first years of friendship; but my notebook reminds me of one attempt: I had just given Wystan a report on a new love, and he, frowning through his Lucky smoke, ventured, "At least, Charlie, your women aren't all the same type," cueing me to declare, "Women are all the same! They're all pink inside!" And while Wystan was chuckling and protesting that there were many shades of pink, I added, "I prefer women with a basic baroque beat!" And Wystan the baroque librettist opined that my preference was both whimsical and sound.

I often heard Wystan and Chester complain about unhappy incidents on Ischia isle until they gladly made the move to Austria. Wystan told me about the cafe on Ischia, where he got his mail and where a clique tried to dominate the island's sexual politics, but his general complaint was that the gay majority there was making his once enchanted isle a neurotic capital. My notebook reveals:

Wystan (scornfully): Tennessee seems to want the whole world to become queer.

Of course Wystan hadn't given up his youthful ideal of an ordered world affording love, family, and creativity, coupled with tolerance for any abnormal minority, a Blakean world of humankind on a manageable planet.

Whenever I went to Wystan's, I was aware of his little cluttered work table near the front windows, and I was glad that the masochistic metropolitan sunlight often touched Wystan's bent shoulders of an afternoon. One day Wystan asked me, "What is your number over there on East Tenth Street?" He shuffled toward his work table: "I want to put it in my address book." He bent over the table, which seemed more trammeled than usual with tides of manuscript, his new

Olivetti portable listing to one side, loose papers ebbing under its edges, like a vessel about to drift away. "Hmmm, it was right here." He began to paw through the papers, and I stood discreetly aside but exclaimed, "There! Isn't that it?" Wystan inserted his hand like a spatula under the biggest pile to turn it right over and then repeated the operation on other piles. We were both into the search; I peered long-sighted but fascinated while Wystan wheezed above the every-which-way heaps of paper, until, "Aaaah!" he triumphantly plucked out the little black book I'd glimpsed at the first churning.

Relieved, justified, Wystan sank into his work chair and squintingly entered my street number and apartment in his book while I stared at the rumpled vista of papers, wondering how Wystan could ever restore it to its original wave pattern. Yet, from such thrilling disorder, Wystan conjured his ordered world of poems, essays, and libretti.

A few days later, the tiny mailbox by my English basement apartment held an embossed invitation to Wystan's fifty-second birthday party, a memorable event.

I asked Wystan if I could bring a friend and he agreed, so I asked Jean Garrigue, a companion poet, who wondered who would be at the party. "Almost everybody," I ventured, knowing Wystan's and Chester's range of friends.

The embossed invitation card read, "At nine," and concluded with fair warning, "Carriages at one," but when Jean and I arrived there well after nine we were alone with Wystan and Chester as they bustled about, preparing the rooms and refreshments. Chester's father, Edward Kallman, a dentist, soon arrived and greeted me warmly, "Yes, I remember you from January 1942, when you were in town and you carried the money to Chester at Wystan's in Ann Arbor." Mr. Kallman was now filled out but not fat, with metropolis-florid face, a healthy alert man, questioning Jean about her latest book of poetry and quizzing me about our mutual friends who had moved from Kallman's Brooklyn neighborhood to my Vermont region. Now Wystan and Chester were putting platters of food and trays of glasses around the rooms, as well as ice buckets for champagne. Wystan had centered a portable table in the main room and loaded it with buffet foods: meats, cheeses, creamed herring, smoked eel, bagels and breads, bowls of fresh raw vegetables—although he and Chester didn't care for such "rabbit food." A guest brought a huge nesselrode cake, which slowly vanished through the hours. Jean introduced me to Bill Meredith and stood talking quietly with him, her face and honey-pink hair shining brightly amid the dark suits of arriving men. Frank O'Hara bounced in, laughing and joking with his usual joy in life.

After ten o'clock, people arrived steadily. George Balanchine came in alone, loquacious and comic as he lustily discussed City Center politics with Wystan and then stepped around the rooms, appraising the guests, a slim and ageless man who seemed as if he might suddenly choreograph the mixed crowd into an impromptu ballet—or perhaps in his mind the crowd already was an impromptu ballet. Jacques Barzun stood, modestly elegant in suit and tie, regarding the swarm of talkers with Gallic calm. Gian Carlo Menotti appeared in black leather jacket and whipcord jodphurs, as if he'd just jumped off a motorcycle or maybe a camel. Elisabeth Niebuhr glowed among the young poets—Jim Schuyler, Frank O'Hara, and others; Lincoln Kirstein showed up in tailored correctness, smiling and shyly aloof while talking almost exclusively with Wystan.

As the rooms filled, Wystan never sat down or stayed long in one spot, but moved around to say a few words with almost every person while he kept tabs on food and drink, playing the genial host, filling goblets with champagne, of which there was plenty. Neither Wystan nor Chester drank to keep pace with their guests, and Chester was noticeably well behaved. There were several would-be witty toasts and loud cheery ones, the cheeriest being, "Wystan! To your next fifty years!" Wystan gave a fleeting grin and gladly drank to that one, his lined face lighting with pleasure. Then he strode off to the kitchen to fetch more smoked eel and another flute of French bread. I asked, "May I help?" and he answered, mock-severely, "Of course you may not. Just enjoy yourself."

Sam Barber made his entrance with a handsome young man; and I, introduced as "Charlie, from Vermont," was quickly questioned about Green Mountain ski slopes, which Barber and his new friend planned to visit.

Lotte Lenya, slim and graceful in party pants, tall in high-heeled dancing clogs, was the supreme female presence, her pink face framed by loose peach-blonde hair; her ultra-blondeness gave her face and neck the charming appearance of blushing when she spoke with friends. And as I watched her eminently ageless face lifted among her admirers, her throat slightly arched and ready, thrushlike, I sighed and refrained from asking her about the young B. Traven she might have known (under any of his aliases) in pre-Nazi Germany.

By the stereo niche, Chester was happily orating on opera to a huddle of his friends and followers, lifting the arm to place the stylus onto a favorite aria. Jean and I stood near Chester when he began to tease an earnest young man with his recent bride; and when those newlyweds left the room, Chester said, "I'm sorry they're so happily married!" and laughed raucously, when one of his followers added, "We trust that they won't stay married very long."

Nabokov's *Lolita* was much discussed, and toward midnight guests gathered around Wystan, talking excitedly, sometimes several at once, about Nabokovian tricks. Chester intoned, "Vivian Darkbloom indeed!" I put in my two bits: "And Quilty's license plate!" Wystan looked at me, hunched his eyebrows, and I explained, "WS 1564–1616." Faces frowned at me, Wystan questioned, "So?" I replied: "William Shakespeare, 1564–1616." They all chuckled over my contributory crumb to the feast. Later, Wystan and I clashed over *Lolita*, as Jean Garrigue and I had done.

Many people came and went. By midnight, Wystan was obviously tired; but when Jean and I made to leave, Chester beckoned to me, whispering loudly, "Hang around! We're having coffee and brandy by and by." Wystan nodded approval, and so we continued to sip champagne, which had promoted my head into upper spheres.

It was three A.M. when, in a daze of coffee, brandy, and

loud voices from the few remaining guests, we left. Wystan was numb with fatigue but affable, shaking our hands, giving Jean a pat on the shoulder. Jean and I walked slowly across the sullen, frigid Village toward her cat-guarded apartment at 4 Jones Street, and Jean declared, "Wystan's party was just what a poet's party ought to be."

A week after the birthday party I had a long talk with Wystan from early tea time to late evening, and I was surprised that following that event Wystan would be home alone, Chester absent, no phone calls or drop-ins, and no plans to go out. But however glum for Wystan, it was my gain, for we had time to talk over a few glasses of wine, as my journal of February 28, 1959, notes:

> Wystan spoke of 1941, when I screamed in my sleep. "You were deeply troubled then, and now you're not. You've learned at least how to live with your mind! Hmmm, your mother, she's uh. . . ." Yes, I told him that she was still going strong at eighty, still baking her own bread, gardening. And still revered as "Mom" by my nine brothers and sisters, all living. We got onto poverty and hunger, as I experienced it in Depression Chicago, but Wystan denied that I could be "still hungry since the Depression," so I spoke again of Depression bread-line days.

Wystan wasn't too interested in the anatomy of hunger, or in my citations from Richard Wright and James Baldwin. Full bellies do not erase the trauma of true physical hunger, and Wystan interrupted to guess that my spiritual hunger caused me to remember my physical hunger. But I was arguing that the underdog's belly has total recall. I remembered, in my guts, how my belly, even when being filled with a rare good Depression meal, braced itself for the next day's hunger—just as the gourmet's belly relaxes for the next filling within the next few hours! Now in the Village I was fairly rich with a wealth of friends, but lived alone in an English basement room at eight dollars a week rent, limiting my food and entertainment to another eight dollars a week, so I could save a large part of my weekly unemployment compensation of forty dollars to pay my Vermont property taxes, mortgage payments on my little home, and other debts. What little I drank was courtesy of friends.

All of my mousey functional poverty was dedicated to my creative efforts, so I felt rich in spirit while continuing to live poor, something of an arrested Depression child. Wystan wanted to understand my stance, and thereby helped me to crystallize it; but still he frowned when I sardonically described how I strolled past Luchow's to sniff plump odors before I turned back to First Avenue markets to buy beans, lentils, cabbage, and day-old pumpernickel to sustain the body that lodges the soul.

Although I felt that Wystan was sincere in his protests against my intentional poverty, it never occurred to me to remind him that his own way of life was related to mine: he lived cheaply on Saint Mark's Place, he ate, dressed, and scrooged in order to be free of social status, social location— while his earnings gestated in a trust investment fund. He was a lonely at the top of the poetry profession, slumming in his beloved Village, from which vantage point he could scan the equivocal outlines of his Just City.

Bless you, darling, I have
Found myself in you.
"Heavy Date"

When Wystan and Chester lived together in their "snug apartment" on Saint Mark's Place, they gave the impression of being a "married couple," and Wystan seemed to encourage this impression, but actually they had a nonconnubial contract, as Chester confided to me. When I first met Wystan he spoke to me of "privacy," pronouncing it with heavy British emphasis, and I soon learned that his "privacy" meant not only sanctuary from intrusion into his creative work hours but shelter from storms of questions concerning his past history, his income, his religious beliefs, and his sexual habits. While he often appeared to be an open, frank person, ever attuned to truth and honesty, there were many aspects of his nature that, like any sensitive person, he wanted to be kept secret. And his true relationship with Chester was a principal secret.

In his poems, Wystan not only revealed and glorified his visions, but he often made his personal idiosyncrasies appealing, in a manner that Eliot, Stevens, Williams, and Lowell could not match. Any reader of Wystan's poems will encounter his warmhearted humanity as well as his philosophical vision; that was his happy paradox.

Perhaps Wystan's deepest "privacy" could be penetrated, his mysteries postulated, by a conclave of family, friends, and lovers, as well as peers and colleagues, from all corners of the compass, but there would remain the human mystery of Wystan Auden as person and poet, a mystery that often eludes words, camera, and canvas: the essence of a complex man. The essence properly pursued by biographers and intimated by memoirists.

When I made notes on Wystan in my journal or discussed him with friends or (best of all) considered him in my mind, it was my attempt to understand him as person, poet, and friend. It wasn't in my nature to be clinical, it never occurred to me to question his friends, much less to question Chester; I listened, I discussed, and at last I knew that it was Chester who, if anyone, held the coveted key to Wystan as person and poet. If the letters of Wystan and Chester come to light in the near future they will reveal mysteries of love and marriage that outsiders can't reveal; for they confided in each other freely, frequently, consistently, as lifelong lovers sometimes do. In Ann Arbor, Wystan "blubbered" (as he said) a few times when he talked on the phone to Chester in New York, and he read to me portions of letters to, as well as from, Chester, letters that rivaled some of the celebrated love poems. Whatever else they may have been, Chester and Wystan were complete confidants.

Chester confided casually in me, as he did in many

friends, and I always found him easy to be with; we never quarreled, and we hardly experienced an unpleasant moment. I listened to Chester by the hour but was seldom bored. From 1940 on, I observed him evolving as student, writer, and poet. After Chester left Ann Arbor in June 1943, he wrote me letters describing his drudgery in New York bureaucracies, his "essential" wartime jobs. He wanted to make his own way, and he did, to some extent, even when he rejoined Wystan's ménage on Saint Mark's Place. And it was there, in 1960, that Chester told me that he was going to migrate from his native New York and "hang out" in Europe, mostly in Athens, except for summer stays with Wystan in Austria.

Chester managed to retain most of his individuality while inhabiting the eye of Wystan's creative storm. Wystan ever encouraged and promoted Chester's creativity and teamed up successfully with him on opera libretti. At Wystan's apartment, Chester told me how Wystan criticized his first manuscript collection of poems and then declared, "Your poems must be published. I think Grove Press might do them." Chester continued: "Wystan asked, 'Do you want to take the manuscript over to Grove Press, or shall I?' So I told Wystan, 'Oh, you might as well do that for me.' So Wystan took the manuscript and gave it to Barney Rosset, saying, 'I think these poems should be published.' And Rosset said, 'Fine! If you say so.' "

My journal notes:

Chester says, "Grove Press so-called Evergreen editions don't stay green, for my book will go out of print as soon as the Evergreen list gets a new title. However, my poems are also in a limited edition with special binding and with an original drawing by Larry Rivers, at fifty bucks. It was snapped up by my friends and family. But most of the edition is in paperback."

I read Chester's poems but wasn't crazy about them, and told him so. He once handed me a libretto manuscript, and while I read it he buzzed around the apartment, reciting his doubts: "I'm afraid it's a flop. I couldn't get with it. It means little to me." With such asides I casually agreed.

In the late 1950s, Chester gave me a typescript of *The Tuscan Players*, which he'd written on commission from Carlos Chavez; and though I couldn't appreciate the libretto I enjoyed Chester's description of an informal Chavez in Mexico City, where Chester stayed at the Maria Cristina Hotel, on Rio Lerma. I had lived at times with friends in a carriage house facing the Maria Cristina; Chester and I had known the same local characters, and I was fond of the area, which reminded me of a mellow Paris *arrondissement*. This connection is a sample of my affinities with garrulous Chester.

One of Chester's best achievements was his collaboration with Wystan on *The Rake's Progress*, scored by Stravinsky; yet, three volumes of poems, various libretti of his own, and translations of others amount to a respectable achievement for the Brooklyn student who had presented himself to Wystan in early 1939.

Obviously, Wystan loved Chester and appreciated his qualities, including Chester's Brooklyn scorn, toughness, and crude sense of humor, as well as his attachment to his very American Jewish family. Wystan eagerly told friends of Chester's accomplishments, both literary and culinary; but I never heard commonsensical Chester bore anyone with recitations of Wystan's public achievements. He spoke of them casually, referring to Wystan's periodic lectures at Oxford in the same tone he used when explaining, "Wystan is upstate, for a reading."

Chester loved all Wystan-lore:

You know, Charlie, our friends kept telling us about these comfortable new "space" shoes, so we went uptown to get a pair for Wystan's sick feet. The shoe clerk was as sweet as he could be but Wystan's feet defied fitting, not only because of his corns and bunions but because his feet are wide at the toes and narrow at the heels. You ought to have seen Wystan in "space" shoes! The only ones he could squeeze into looked like three-pound pumpernickel loaves! He clumped around the store—I couldn't stop giggling—he sat down and said, "I *won't* wear them!" He put his carpet slippers on and went home.

Chester told me how Wystan went through a glass door:

You saw the warning stripe of red paint on the glass entry door, down there? Notice that the glass is new, also. Wystan started down the stairs the other night, high as a gull, and I soon heard a great crash. I ran to the stair landing and looked down to see him picking himself up from a pile of broken glass. "Are you all right?" I called, and he answered very distinctly, "Ya-as, my dear, but I cut my finger!"

Chester, gurgling happily, went on: "You know how *huge* Wystan is getting! He always was clumsy, but now he's clumsy as a bear. Could *you* pass through a glass door like that?"

No, I couldn't. But I could imagine Wystan galumping toward the glass, hitting it with forehead, knees, and shoulder, all at once. And knowing the strength of plate glass, I figured that he had knocked the great five-foot pane of glass from the weathered wooden door, so that it fell onto the terra cotta entry floor, breaking, with Wystan on top of it, as I told Chester, who laughed and said, "Wystan was not only on *top* of it, he was with it!"

My journal notes Chester telling on himself:

"The boys are saying that I'm not *really* queer! This has got to stop." Deadpan, I didn't stop listening, but could hardly restrain my laughter when Chester, very serious, told me how he defended his "queerness" to some Kallman-tribe girls who visited the apartment: "This biggest slob of a girl, she wanted to know right off, 'What for's all that vaseline by your bed?' And I told her right off, 'It's not for you, big girl!' "

Thus Chester made himself plain to visitors, friends, and family, showing a clown face, just as Wystan often did; but behind Chester's Brooklyn guise was a genuine minor poet who published metric riddles, clues to his long relationship with Wystan. For Chester was, after all, the American mate, the permanent problem mate, of an Old World master who quested for love and friendship in our wide open society, our New World, and found it, if ambiguously, in Chester Kallman.

NINE

He hears a loudspeaker
Call him well-known;
But knows himself no better.
"Iceland Revisited"

WHILE I CONTINUED TO ENJOY GREAT TALKS WITH WYSTAN IN the sixties, I paid less attention to his poetry than to his person; and this pleased Wystan, who saw his work as separate from his person. When *Homage to Clio* was published in 1960, I was among the many who saw little to excite in the volume; rather, as I recall, I searched for the Auden of the thirties and forties in his poetry of the late fifties. One poet said to me, with lively rancor, "Auden's last *good* poem was 'In Praise of Limestone,'" which was published in 1948; and while I couldn't agree with such a judgment, I did hope for Wystan's return in spirit and inspiration to such previous triumphs as the Yeats poem, or the comprehensive and startling Freud poem, or the nimble, juxtapositional thrills of *New Year Letter*.

After admiring *The Age of Anxiety* for the eloquence Wystan put into the mouths of four unmemorable human figures, I enjoyed the wit, wisdom, humanity, and music that graced the long poem. But I, along with too many other readers, was committing a common idealistic sin of asking the artist to assume a role desired by the reader rather than letting the artist act out his own creative role.

Although Wystan's American republic of readers may have withered away a bit in the sixties, he was gaining new followers around the world with new poems and with some of his Oxford lectures published as essays in *The Dyer's Hand*; his *Collected Shorter Poems* and his *Collected Longer Poems* were scheduled for publication on both sides of the Atlantic. His discerning followers and critics could agree with the English critic G. S. Fraser, who judged "Auden, the composite giant . . . whose composite voice, or tonality, is viable on both sides of the Atlantic . . . to bestride the Atlantic like a colossus."*

At home, Wystan never in my hearing discussed the critical reception of his books, but we often discussed our favorite authors. One evening I described to him my "discovery" that Thomas Hardy was a "hair freak." Wystan seemed startled and instantly demanded textual proof, so I first cited the centerpiece, or hair piece, in *The Woodlanders*, where the novel's plot is hung by Hardy strands on Marty South's auburn hair; and I cited from memory the long soliloquy in a Hardy story where the narrator sits in view of a lovely woman's hairdo: "What a work of art! To think of doing up the hair like that for an occasion, yes, but to think of doing it up like that *every day!*"

Wystan never discussed Melville but remarked many times that "*Moby Dick* is really an epic poem, and should be read that way," tending not to examine Melville but to enshrine him. Wystan got me to read Verga's *House by the Medlar Tree*, and he spoke of the clear, concise delineation of Sicilian social structure as Verga outlined it in details of family, church, and village life (a tiny Sicilian "whole view," I noted). Wystan concluded, "It seems incredible that so much misfortune could overtake one family, but we know it *can* happen that way."

Generally, Wystan was a genial judge of contemporary

* "Auden: The Composite Giant," *Shenandoah* 15, no. 4 (Summer 1964).

poets and writers; he was too civil to entertain mean opinions of creative writers, choosing to climax a discussion with a shrug, "Hmmm, that poet is *not* to my taste." There was a galaxy of good writers very much to Wystan's taste, and one of them was Vincent Van Gogh, whom we quoted and discussed, after I declared, "Van Gogh is a great writer!" Wystan challenged me, "A great *writer*?" And I said, in effect, "His letters are great because they create for me a whole world I would not otherwise know, and they recreate people whom I can visualize as if they stood before me, all kinds of individuals in the round—life!" Actually, Van Gogh's life haunted me, his ideal relationship with his brother Theo, his drive for full expression, his restless search for a good life—well, a decent life—in which to create art; his whole life a quest with minimal rewards, a life that I felt was related to my own anarchic quest. "Some publisher ought to publish all of Van Gogh's letters!" I finished doggedly.

"All of them? Not too likely. There are too many. But good selections have been published," Wystan assured me, for he himself had edited a selection. (Were Wystan alive today he could enjoy most of Van Gogh's letters in new definitive editions.)

During my repeated stays in Manhattan I often spent long evenings in the public library reading rooms on Fifth Avenue and Forty-Second Street; and there one wintry night when I sat deep in the "Even" reference room with books and writing pad before me, along with scholars, students, readers, and loafers of all ages from many lands, I looked up to spot Wystan striding slowly through the ranks of crowded tables, on his way over to the "Odd" room. He did a scholar's stooping imitation of Groucho Marx—rather, Groucho used to do a stoop-stride imitation of gangly scholars like Wystan. He was wearing his old brown tweed overcoat and carrying a nondescript briefcase and clutching an old tome to his heart. It was natural to see him there in his forest of books, hunting for information, slouching past the OED and Webster's Unabridged toward more elusive game. No one seemed to recognize him, no one greeted him or started up to confront him with a question, any more than they did on Saint Mark's Place or along the open market stalls of First Avenue near his "nest." Yes, Wystan belonged to the Public Library, to New York, and certainly to the Lower East Side: Sutton Place or Central Park West wouldn't suit him. Not at all.

> *Lions came loping into the*
> *lighted city.*
> "For the Time Being"

In the fall of 1961 I came to Wystan's one tea time to find my poet a gray-faced ghost of the energetic young creator of earlier decades. He sat in a lumpy chair, fumbling for a cigarette as he turned his leonine head to give me a quick, questioning glance that passed like slow-motion radar through cloud-wisps of cigarette smoke before his furrowed face. I recall thinking that Wystan was a male Medusa, that my soul was in danger of turning to stone, to salt, or to molten lava; that Wystan might contrive (like my older evil brothers) to destroy me: yet at that very black magical moment, Wystan said, in his cosmopolitanized Yorkshire voice, "Well, Charlie, what are you up to?"

I was up to visiting Wystan, to bringing him good news, for a change: I'd spent months in England and Europe (I'd visited John Ashbery in Paris, as Wystan had prompted me to do); I'd stayed in an abandoned château in Provence for two months, sponsored by Jean Giono. And I'd returned on the last westward voyage of the *Liberté*, with good expectations for a better, or more solvent, life; for my house in Vermont had been sold, and my debts paid off. I'd written much, and some of it was scheduled for publication, although my poetic novel, *Bricklayer*, lay abandoned when my editor at McGraw-Hill jumped to another publisher and answered none of my last letters.

"Will you go back to your Pullman apartment on East Fifty-Third Street?" Wystan wondered. (I had given him a dinner there in late spring when we were both about to leave Manhattan.) Wystan had liked the apartment and had mentioned his old place on East Fifty-Second. No, I wouldn't stay in Manhattan, I told him, but, "in a month or so I'm going to Mexico, where the living is easy," where, as I'd once written him, "I have the luck and ability to live on beans."

Wystan sat in his chair and traveled vicariously to Africa by way of Joy Adamson's books on her lions, as he read passages from the books to me. He was especially impressed with the lioness Elsa's loyalty to her human hosts, returning to their compound after months of freedom on the veldt, and again after whelping her cubs. Wystan turned the pages to read to me the description of George Adamson's killing and quartering meat for the tame young lioness. And while Wystan hunched forward in his chair, engrossed in real lions, I marveled at his pure worship of books: he had no pictures or statuettes of lions, or of any other beast, in his home, for his favorite art objects were endless lines of words—ordered, unsecretive hieroglyphs that rendered up rounded images, whole dimensions, to be programmed into his mind. He devoured language the way Elsa devoured dead cows; he was crammed with cognitive treasure: Why feel sorry for this treasure-glutted wordsmith?

As soon as Wystan put down the Adamson book, he spoke eagerly of the bear cubs I'd kept in Michigan in late 1942, the cubs he'd missed seeing on a hasty return trip to Ann Arbor. Well, as I told him, the charming cubs of 1942 quickly grew into the hairy hulks of 1943, and I'd exiled them to a bear keeper before they had time to devour me; but I did hand him two snapshots which showed the cubs nuzzling my overalls for a handout of candy.

I knew that Wystan hadn't had my earthy advantages ("I was reared with plants and relative beasts," as my "Origins" says), but he had graduated from his boyhood love of beasts as ambulant toys, as strong-odored, purring charmers with eloquent tails, and now regarded them as warm-blooded fellow creatures reared in a purer world than our society: wordless ambassadors of jungle and forest, mortal artifacts of myth and history.

In the thirties, Wystan wrote, ". . . Lion griefs loped from the shade / And on our laps their muzzles laid," and, when we lived together in Ann Arbor, ". . . Lions came loping into the lighted city." These are samples of Wystan's bestiary, for which a good epitaph might be his Brueghelian lines, ". . . the dogs go on with their doggy life and the torturer's horse / Scratches its innocent behind on a tree."

Wystan had met one of my dogs, a sensitive and intelligent Dalmatian that visited and charmed him at his Cornelia Street digs; but now he was eager to hear and rehear reports on Carlito, my black and white monkey in Mexico, an Atelus male that squatted on my shoulder when I walked in the village and wrapped his snakey arms around my neck when we rode standing in third-class buses. This monkey had a blotch of black fur cocked on the white fuzz of his head like a Yucatan yarmulke, and he was obsessed with trying to type on my typewriter, even while I advised him not to join the human race. ("It's too violent, too many taxes, too much social pressure for any decent monkey.") Once my monkey sprayed B. Traven with a can of insecticide, doubly insulting the reclusive jungle man who had befriended other monkeys before he befriended mine. Wystan was ready to laugh at the exploits of my Carlito, a monkey who chattered much and hardly knew how to laugh.

Even though Wystan wasn't his old puckish self, he never lost flashes of that self. He was fond of talking about "the old days," and we shared private references to the past; not necessarily to his "ilk," but to any ilk. Wystan once asked me, "Do you remember Don Whiting from Ann Arbor? No? He remembers you!" And I replied: "No, I can't quite remember him—there were so many of *them* and only one of *me*!" Wystan relished this kind of smart aleckry, though he seldom employed it in his own speech.

Chester's absence made a difference in Wystan's home life, causing him increased loneliness and a sense of loss. When he wrote, "I can't miss what I no longer need," that is, sex and regular companionship, I wanted to believe him; but he was, in fact, desperately lonely, as older and sickly persons can be. Although his "snug apartment in New York" was trespassed by loneliness, it was still his home, hearth, nest, studio, and office, where the clutter varied with seasons and times. Visitors made comments about the disorder, but it was no more disordered or cluttered than, say, Picasso's studio; "squares" take pleasure in cataloging heaps of half-used paint tubes, mounds of sculptors' chips, drifts of writers' notepaper, but these are only the excretia that accompany creation. Over the years, Wystan altered pathways through his poet-spoor without disturbing its distinctive dishevelment. The old sofa sagged downward like a beached lifeboat, the coffee table kept its place, loaded, and the lumpy chairs were not dislodged.

But, alas, Wystan's cats were dislodged. When Chester left in 1961, Wystan could hardly cope with his two cats because of his travels, and no friends volunteered to vacation them. So it was a shock to me when Wystan the animal lover finally felt obliged "to put them to sleep."

In October 1961 I came to Wystan's and was admitted by a huge and expressive Negro maid who dawdled among accumulations of boxes, bags, and cases in the front room while Wystan sat in weary grandeur, wearing an elegant if soiled purple-striped shirt while he surveyed the scene. He had recently arrived from Europe, and the room looked like a portion of Pier 19 with his suitcases, cartons, and tottering towers of twine-tied books covering most foot passage in the room. An enticing stack of wine cases waited near his knee.

It was quickly apparent that the maid was not only new to Wystan but had preceded me by a few hours, for, after a half-sentence introduction ("Charlie, this, uh, is Maud"), she continued briefing Wystan, who had just returned from uptown: "Yeah, like ah tole you, this fella he came right on in, like he belong here, he say he's your good friend, and he say *you* tole *him* to taka bottla this heah wine, like you got so many. Yeah, like you *owed* it to *him*, see!" Maud delivered this speech with dramatic gusto, standing knee deep in the assembled clutter, gesturing and pointing, orating as if her future depended on our verdict. We listened in admiration of this huge and black personage, and I had a feeling that we might be listening to her for hours, for Wystan was fascinated by her elocutionary powers. Finally, with a wisp of smoke invading his right eye, he softly growled from the cave of his hangover, enunciating with toughness: "Don't give 'em nothin'! Nothin' to anybody!"

Maud, relieved, roared with laughter, shaking the premises, wagging her head knowingly, chuckling as divas chuckle for theaters of ears, "Nuthin' to nobody! Aw right, ah'm givin' nuthin' to nobody, from now on!" She continued wading and waddling through the boxes and bags, mumbling loudly to herself, "But ah don' see how ah kin *clean* anything aroun' heah till all this *stuff* is *cleaned* outta th' way!"

Wystan gave me a commiserating wink, sank back in his old chair and put one of his big feet atop a convenient wine case: "This wine was a good buy, but I must guard every bottle of it." He waved his cigarette at the cases, "All reserved for, uh, entertainment purposes." He squinted at me through low-hanging cigarette haze, as I instantly experienced my old recurring suspicion of Audenian orgies: the apartment echoing with squealing boys, weary musicians, deferential poets and painters buzzing with Wystan's communal Bacchanal wine. Such orgies probably existed only in my Freudian suspicion and not in fact.

The wine Wystan had bought was mostly French red, some of it Bordeaux Médoc, all of it packed in thin white-pine board boxes, each mouthwatering bottle couched on crisp golden excelsior, simple but elegant white château labels hugging the dark bottles. With a sigh, Wystan summoned Maud to bring two glasses from the kitchen so we could taste a bottle of fruity, full-bodied vintage, a rich relative of the California Pinot Noir of Ann Arbor days.

We talked a bit about everything that winey early afternoon, relaxed after Maud's performance, but it was clear to me that wine was now one of Wystan's best friends, and this recently arrived vintage gave him its best in lonely liquid friendship.

> ... *Yours the choice to whom the gods*
> *The language of learning, the language*
> *of love.*
> "A Bride in the 30s"

Whenever I visited Wystan in the sixties I was impressed with his loneliness, but concluded that it was possible for so considerable a figure, so charming a person, to be chronically lonely and alone because he was basically an asocial man. Since Ann Arbor days I had noticed that Wystan could, at times, enjoy social occasions with colleagues, peers, and friends of his own ilk, but his compulsion to work guaranteed his loneliness. In earlier days Wystan spoke often, to me and other unproved poets, about fame, talent, and diligence. "Fame is an accident," he said, but "accomplishment through exercise of one's talent is no accident," and when it came to exercise of talent Wystan proved that he wasn't accident prone. In addition to being a "private person," and a solitary creator, Wystan was, like one in any ten persons, an overt homosexual, and thus a minority of one in the minority Third Sex.

Sometimes I saw Wystan surrounded by men of his own ilk, and I was surprised that he sometimes appeared to be bored—bored perhaps as a man can sometimes be with his wife and family, no matter how loved; or perhaps bored like an Eastern potentate with his harem. But he never seemed to be bored with Chester, even when Chester foraged for love elsewhere (seaward, when possible).

Love was the greatest force in Wystan's complex life, and his writings prove it; but his greatest hunger was for beauties of the mind, for creation, for communion with spirits living and departed; and this hunger was fairly well fulfilled.

Chester had his own reasons for retaining a measure of freedom, for fighting for his own individuality; he had made known to me that Wystan was less than a satisfactory sexual lover. Chester's friends had hinted to me of "Wystan's clumsiness," his "ineptness." One of Chester's clinical friends claimed, "Chester taught Wystan half of what little he knows about sex," and I instantly discounted this biased claim, though it may have some truth in it. A future member of the Third Sex may sometime present the clinical sex clubs of the world with the super porno-saintly truth of Wystan's none-too-secret sex life, complementing the lavish clues he left in his poems.

The Wystan I knew best was the most generous Wystan, endowed with large humanity, with empathy and understanding of a whole world, the person he claimed to be in our first hour on Pontiac Trail, "normal in every way but the sexual."

Any study of human sexuality can become complex, but, in Wystan's case, the fact is clear that he quested for "commonality" in America (as he had in Berlin and elsewhere), that he was ever attracted to persons who were not his peers, and usually younger men; that this questing tendency was, perhaps, related to his rejection of older, more evil, more complex Europe in favor of our (supposedly) less evil, more simple, young America. Aside from his personal sexuality, Wystan stands in his work on a firm and real earth with a clear vision of "the human condition," with few phobias, few fantasies. Like many complex creators, he "had it both ways," for he inhabited two worlds, the whole and the abnormal (even if he cohabited mostly in the latter); and this ability to inhabit two worlds is part of the fascination Wystan Auden holds for his readers.

Once in Wystan's "other" world at the City Center Ballet, I turned aside when he beckoned to me in the lobby, where he stood talking with Dag Hammarskjold, for I felt too "shy" to join them. Wystan let my self-conscious lapse go by without reproof, for later that week he told me about his interesting conversation with "Dag." Seeing Wystan with the self-effacing secretary general of the United Nations was a treat: the World Legislator with the World Poet. It was known in New York that the World Legislator, smiling faintly to conceal his shyness (a kind of uncomic young Charlie Chaplin), admired the metrics of the World Poet; so I was pleased that I had side-stepped the two bachelor bards talking guardedly to each other—perhaps about world poetry and the evening's occasion, the world premiere of the lavish new ballet *Medea*.

One day I came to the flat to find Wystan shuffling about more like an old auntie than I'd ever seen him, and with a rare note of complaint: "You know, uh, they had to change it, to, ummm, Audenstrasse, hummmph!" And off he grunted to the kitchen to fill our coffee cups. I had to listen carefully to get this much, postulating that Wystan's village lane in Kirchstetten had been renamed Audenstrasse. "Well!" I said while Wystan hobbled back from the kitchen, saying more clearly (as if he had inserted his dentures while in the kitchen!), "Hmmm, they could have left it the way it was, during my lifetime. People will be bothering me, now. Please tell me, Charlie, how I must react when I'm obliged to give my address as 'Audenstrasse'?"

Cheerfully, I said, "Come off it, Wystan! There must be other streets named after you in other places on earth."

And Wystan, quick as a chuckle, suddenly became affable. "If so, I shan't be obliged to live on them!"

He was obviously pleased as well as embarrassed with this new honor, so I told him that when I had visited Jean Giono in Manosque, France, in his modest house on "Chemin Giono," he had seemed able to live very well with the signpost honor. Wystan sniffed, his face lighted up. "Aaah, Giono! Do you like his novels as well as those of Verga?"

I began to discuss some of Giono's provincial alpine novels, leaving Audenstrasse in its own place.

When *The Dyer's Hand* was published in 1962, I was out of the country, I didn't buy the book, and I talked with few persons who read it; but it was clear that this excellent book caused less excitement among poetry buffs than a book of Wystan's poems would have caused. My own limited and often long-distance circle neglected the book of essays; even Jean Garrigue and Mark Van Doren, with whom I often discussed Wystan's work, assumed that *The Dyer's Hand* marked another notch in, as Jean called it, "Auden's decline." Of course Wystan said nothing about the book when I saw him, as was his habit, for he was busy on other, newer projects—essays, introductions, reviews, translations, edited collections; and he was chronically accepting lecture offers, if not seasonal tours. The flood of poetry had slackened to a trickle, and the last decade of his life saw a faint—though firm—reflection of former decades. As for *The Dyer's Hand*, I wasn't the only Auden follower to harvest its richness after the frost.

In the sixties a young provincial poet wrote me, "I'm going down to New York where I hope to view the Auden ruins." This indicated the attitude of many Auden followers across the nation, mixing their vision of Wystan's person with his poetry. This provincial poet was the only writer I ever represented to Wystan, carrying his manuscript of poems to Wystan and discussing them, but to no avail, for the poems didn't take with Wystan; and later I saw the manuscript dwelling in the dungeon of a closed cabinet in Wystan's front room. Wystan read, "discovered," and awarded many young poets in the Yale Series of Young Poets; but those were official discoveries, not friends' promotions.

Wystan's poetry, a marriage of the prophetic and the lyrical, never deserted vision; and one of my favorites among his young visionary poems is "A Summer Night," a prophecy of later works. Its opening lines are crisply, purely lyric: "Out on the lawn I lie in bed, / Vega conspicuous overhead / In the windless nights of June . . . / my feet / Point to the rising moon." But as this celebration of nominal solitude in company continues, the poet lets his "whole view" take over, so that his universal compassion marks the poem like a mission— the Auden mission—a hope for community of spirit, for love and order in our warring century. The singer gives way in this poem to the stern prophet, warning his world; but, as Wystan aged, his political prophecies waned, and he became impeccably apolitical, opposed to the demagogism of any party.

As for young prophetic poets arriving on the scene, Wystan was wary; and I recall a heated discussion of Allen Ginsberg's *Howl*, during which Wystan declined to agree with Chester's negative appraisal. And in the late sixties, Wystan said in my hearing, "Of course Allen *has* contributed to literature. *Howl does* have much to say, and Allen may well grow to even larger achievements. Give him time."

Once in the sixties I came to Wystan's at tea time to find him surrounded by a group of young people, one of them a worker from Dorothy Day's Catholic Worker Farm, then located on Staten Island. When I started to leave, Wystan said to me, aside, "Sorry it's so congested around here. Why don't you come around to luncheon tomorrow?"

I got there at five to one, safely ahead of his habitual one P.M. lunch hour, but the door opened on a distraught and weary poet who spoke with an obvious hangover in tones as cross as I'd heard in decades: "Charlie, I just got through work. Why don't you come back later?"

"How much later? Could I take you out to lunch?"

"Luncheon? You came for luncheon? Uh . . ."

"Yes. You invited me yesterday. But maybe tomorrow would be better?"

"Hmmm. I did invite you? But I should have shopped. And, Charlie, you might have phoned!"

"It was just yesterday—but we don't have to have lunch . . ."

"Sit down, Charlie! It'll be a simple luncheon. No complaining now!"

I sat on the sofa and read newspapers while Wystan shuffled to the kitchen in his carpet slippers, his shirttails hanging over baggy, unclean pants, a Eugene O'Neill character mumbling over pots and pans. He came out to hand me a periodical opened to an essay on "U" and non-"U" people by Nancy Mitford, as I recall. While I dutifully browsed the article, Wystan came back to see that I was reading it while he questioningly read my face. I shrugged, "It means little to me, probably because I'm not in society."

Wystan frowned, murmured, "Hmmm, not in society, hmmm." I knew that my lack of interest in "U" and non-"U" disappointed him, even while I marveled at his own interest in such gimmicks of society.

Within a half-hour, Wystan brought in a loaf of French bread, a pot of small boiled potatoes, steamed sausages, and a jar of commercial mustard. (Ah, where were "the *real* European mustards" of yesteryear?) He clanked a six-pack of cheap American beer onto the table, hastily opening a can and gulping from it, proving to me that it was his first drink of the day; and I shuddered to think of the American beer additives draining into his sickly stomach. We ate, Wystan voraciously, I pickily. "Doesn't it taste *good* when one is so *hungry*," mumbled Wystan, chomping another sausage, forking butter onto his potatoes. It was a drinker's lunch, no salad, no vegetable except potato, not even the pickle of a "ploughman's lunch." But the bread and potatoes were good, and I drank one beer to Wystan's two. He brought in a metal pot of strong black coffee, lacing his as usual with cream and sugar, sipping it loudly, and then leaning back with a contented sigh. He perked up, even smiled, as we sat, relaxed, and talked about Mexico, Austria, and other places.

Wystan got onto (of all things) electric vehicles: "There were electric automobiles in earlier years. And they worked. They were of use to many people. But it seems that the giant industrialists forced them off the market. Cities like Los Angeles, Chicago, and Houston, which are fairly level and are plagued with gas smog, should subsidize electric vehicles."

I agreed, telling about the Stanley Steamer, "A marvelous motor," which I'd seen in Michigan in the twenties. Wystan's face lit up. Yes, he'd seen a steam motor car, somewhere in his past. So I recalled the electric motor car used in Ann Arbor when Wystan lived there: an old lady on Oxford Road was seen frequently driving her black electric coupe, sitting sedately at the lever controls, guiding her "odorless and noiseless staid little electric brougham," as Wystan described one such vehicle in a poem. Now, he was glad that I invoked a real electric brougham over our coffee.

Finally Wystan gave a glance at his work table and sighed. I got up, and he lit another Lucky, to stoke up for work.

I had experienced other meals at number 77, but none so purely Wystan (so non-U?) as this. In my ninety minutes there, the phone didn't ring, no one came to the door; and I marveled that Saint Mark's peace should so prevail, that Wystan could live so casually in lower-class comfort, so apart from his place out there in libraries, bookstores, periodicals, publications, and airwaves around the world. Here, the sausage-loving, kipper-seeking commoner was in his own world; his mind was one world, his daily life another, as it can be, as it should be. Once he looked up from a conversation and said abruptly, "I found some decent kippers at a new fishmonger's," in the same tone that he might have said, "I stumbled across an incredible Icelandic saga, whose existence I hadn't imagined." Now he sat thinking, half-turned toward his work table, wheezing gently, getting ready to hoist his raffish hulk from the food on the table to that higher nourishment on paper, a few grunts away.

"Wystan! Let me do the dishes!"

"Of course *not*! After all, my deah, I *did* invite you to luncheon!"

> *The God of love*
> *Will never withdraw our right*
> *To grief and infamy.*
> "Symmetries and Asymmetries"

Often in the sixties, when I was alone in Latin America or Europe, far from Wystan, I thought of him sitting at that table in his front room, his back to the Manhattan smogscape, his head inclined over notebook and paper while he continued his long trek down interminable lines of words that led to the fullest expression of his universal awareness. At times, reading Wystan's late flights of imagination and hang-glides over different areas of philosophy, as in his 1968 "Ode to Terminus," I marveled at his feat of living on various levels at the same time. Wystan loved the lower levels, as Shakespeare loved them (and as Dickens reveled in them); he melded the high and the low in his poetry more satisfyingly than did other modern poets.

It isn't easy to know the exact train of thought that leads to the core of an artist's achievement. We do know Wystan's "climate of opinion," his areas of highest interest, and we know that he lived a tremendous inner life, as he expressed it in wide-ranging poems. When Wystan wrote, in 1969, "I feel most at home with what is real," he must have believed it; but when a good reader examines the high intellectual content (or intent) of most of the poems, he may well wonder at the poet's declaration. Certainly he stood on the Real and sighted the Invisible, aware of the nature of both, for his poems make the Invisible very Real. I always felt that when Wystan said "real," he referred to a proven, traditional reality, be it Village politics or Greek drama.

Over the years I was certain that Wystan's poor health was attributable as much to his creative labors as to his waiving of good diet and exercise, and to his obsessive smoking. I also thought that his furrowed face of later years reflected the agonies of writing; that time totted up the price of poetry on his face, that he pursued life—tried to corner it on squares of paper—until life turned and clawed his face. Yet Wystan had no patent on his geopoetic facial map, for here in highland Massachusetts I see a farm woman whose face has identical dermal diagrams, and I see similar anxiety acrostics on the faces of Asian refugees. And recently Jacques Barzun, a friend and literary associate of Wystan's, wrote me: "It may interest you to know that the peculiar gouging of Wystan's facial skin is part of a medical condition known as the Touraine-Solente-Golé syndrome, which also afflicted Racine. I would never have dared mention the fact to Wystan, who disliked Racine and in fact had little use for French literature in general."

So, after all, it is easier to diagnose the Real face of a poet than to chart the Invisible workings of his mind!

Wystan no longer traveled about the world as he did during the thirties, but he liked to travel vicariously to Mexico, which was now my second home; and I gave him good accounts of my adventures on horseback in the central highlands and my later beachcombing episodes on the Pacific coast, where I became a familiar (and well-accepted) gringo in a fishing village. Once I spent an evening hour describing to Wystan the pet deer that played on Los Gatos Beach. It was a small buck with milk-chocolate brown hairs interlaid with gray-white, and it had lost one horn, but it loved to threaten with the remaining horn and to wrestle with anyone who cared to grapple with the single horn (I *had* wanted so much to see a unicorn). "Wystan, it was the only unicorn I ever knew, and a real one!"

When I began, in the sixties, to publish essays on B. Traven's Mexican books, Wystan said, "A fellow anarchist, huh?" B. Traven was a benevolent anarchist, distantly comparable to Thoreau; but I hadn't labeled myself an anarchist until Wystan obliged, and I continued to wear the label in ambiguous faith, for I had devoted myself to avoiding the urban-industrial stampede, just as Traven and Thoreau did.

Wystan could accept B. Traven as author and man because Traven was apolitical, if passionate in warring against all dictators and militarists. Wystan could shrug off Jack London and Maxim Gorki, asserting that I liked their books because those authors came from "the lower depths," not having to assert that he didn't like them because they got involved in politics. He could have added that those two raffish radicals were not genuine artists and that (crowning sin) they could be boring at times. Wystan approved my devotion to Thomas Hardy and suggested I pay more attention to Henry James, his favorite American mentor. But B. Traven was closer to my American reality than were Henry James or T. S. Eliot.

In the spring of 1967 I came to New York for a few days from my residence grant at the Newberry Library in Chicago, and when I came to Wystan's apartment, *The Night Visitor*, a volume of Traven stories, was on the coffee table with no other books. I was gratified to see it there, for I'd edited the stories and written the introduction but had refrained from sending Wystan a copy of the published book.

"Well! Did you like the stories?" I demanded.

Wystan picked up the book and pawed through the pages, mumbling, "Hmmm. Yes. I liked most of the first-person stories, as well as 'Macario.' " He leaned forward in his chair, juggling a cigarette toward the heaped ashtray. "Yes. Certain of the stories gave me a good idea of what the real Mexico must be like." I felt fully rewarded for my labors in Traven's vineyard.

As always, Wystan was interested in my latest adventures in Mexico and incredulous when I told him that my income was less than three hundred dollars a year. "But it certainly costs you a lot of money to travel, and you seem to be on the road often enough, Charlie!"

"Look. I got a ride from Chicago to New York with Traven's niece, and I'm driving an AACON car back to Chicago to its owner. I hitchhike back to Mexico. Easily done." I grinned from my sunburnt vantage point. "But I must admit that the Newberry grant of a thousand dollars puts me way over my own poverty level, for this year." What I didn't admit to Wystan was that I'd met Lynn Perry at the Newberry in Chicago and that I suspected my life was about to change radically, for she tentatively planned to return with me to Mexico.

Wystan sat pondering. Over the decades I never asked for or hinted that I needed any kind of financial aid; in 1958, Wystan had recommended me for a stay at the MacDowell Colony, and that was the sum total of his patronage. I guessed what he was thinking now and was pleased when he said, as my journal noted:

"Now, Charlie, your Spanish must be good enough
to understand the author's intention, and there are

Spanish works that need translating. Do it in your own way, 'after Lorca,' or 'after Octavio Paz.' A decent translation is a good service to readers who might not otherwise read the work in its original language. Now, Charlie, when you get to Texas, go to the International Translation Center in Austin, tell the director I sent you, and they'll give you a project, if you don't already have one of your own in mind. They do have money and they'll give you a grant, if a small one. But it'll help you."

Months later I did get to the International Translation Center, under quixotic circumstances on the last lap of my honeymoon with Lynn. When we were shown into the director's office (then housed in a picturesque former residence at campus edge), there was Wystan smiling dazedly from a blown-up photo of the party celebrating the Center's founding: most of the founders and supporters looked happily tipsy, none more so than Wystan, their goblets of cheer tilted at telltale angles. While the energetic director listened to and approved my project of translating some neglected Mexican literature, I glanced past my young bride's fresh young profile to meet Wystan's photoed smirk, pickled onto his striated face, happy fellow among translators of word and bottle. Their celebration and my grant helped Lynn and me to hitch onward into our adventure-filled future.

Over the years, Wystan spoke to me at times about what used to be called the "servant problem," now not a problem since servants are practically nonexistent. When Wystan and I made our casual verbal contract in Ann Arbor in 1941, I hadn't any feeling that I was a servant, for I felt that we were sharing a house along with its lessee responsibilities; but I once heard Wystan remark, "Americans don't like to serve, so they are unsatisfactory servants." In Ann Arbor, Wystan spoke of our "sharing a house," and although later in letters to friends he spoke of me as his cook, he presented me to Benjamin Britten, Peter Pears, Elizabeth Mayer, and Erika Mann as "my friend, Charlie." I realized that his own thinking was ambiguous, but this didn't bother me.

At Saint Mark's Place, Wystan once handed me a typescript of "Balaam and His Ass: The Servant Problem in Literature," which later appeared in *The Dyer's Hand*, and I remember his manner in handing it to me: he expected me to read it right in front of him, so he could read my face, my reactions. I began to read and soon encountered the phrase "a wet nurse is not a servant, a cook may be." This phrase stopped my reading as I began to muse on Wystan's reason for handing me the typescript. He was staring at me, fascinated, excited by the ideas in his own printed words, as he got up from his chair and started toward the kitchen to bring more coffee, but he stopped in the doorway to watch me—not because it was me, but because he wanted reaction to his words. I read onward, but with difficulty, for I had started thinking about our Ann Arbor discussions of Quixote and Sancho Panza, and with that illustrious duo superimposed on the typescript, I couldn't concentrate. Wystan sighed audibly, having wished to draw fire, or spark, from this failed servant. When he came back with the coffee, I put the typescript aside, one more bit of evidence to add to our many unfinished discussions. But later I wrote him from Vermont my querulous reactions to the essay he had given me.

In my notebook I jotted some of Wystan's phrases from this master–servant essay: "The needs which are satisfied by a master–servant relationship are purely social and historical." And, "A contract . . . differs from a law." And, finally, "It is impossible for a servant, whether he be friendly, hostile or indifferent, not to know exactly what his master is like, for the master reveals himself every time he gives an order." Wystan quoted in this essay the proverb "No man is a hero to his own valet"; but I felt apart, not being his valet, hardly being a servant, not really being under orders from "master" Wystan. Yet I was fascinated that Wystan included my image in his considerations of the master–servant problem. Had I been a prophetic diarist I would have jotted down, in those early days, a helpful sentence from the same essay:

> To present artistically a human personality in its full depth, its inner dialectic, its self-disclosure and self-concealment, through the medium of a single character is almost impossible.

Then, I couldn't foresee that I as failed servant and failed poet was fated—chosen by history—to write, with some help from companion observers, a memoir of a fulfilled poet.

In late 1969, Lynn and I left a troubled Mexico to settle in the sedate part of Massachusetts I'd admired since Cummington School days, and there in the hills west of Greenfield we found ourselves a nineteenth-century farmhouse with barns, a brook, and a few acres of tillable soil to challenge my work ethic. Having nothing better to do with the tiny nest egg of cash we'd saved from making documentary films in Mexico, we founded a personal bookstore (World Eye Bookshop), which rewarded our large devotion with a small living. Our few acres produced some fruit, vegetables, and hay; we raised hens, ducks, rabbits, and goats; we kept a horse and a pony. And in September 1970, our son Lark was born on a Saturday a few hours after Lynn closed the store.

"Dear me, you're now a solid citizen!" said Wystan when I phoned him the news (not saying that we'd debated calling our son Wystan, but we had decided, finally, not to lay *that* on his innocent head). "Yes, Wystan, we're as solid as the mortgage on the farm, the mountain of debt on our little bookshop. We're hooked, we're good Americans!"

We were busy ones, with Lynn alone in the farmhouse while I tended shop. Lynn nursed our child and tended the animals, and I cut wood for the kitchen stove and fireplace, making apple wine as I had done years before on a Connecticut homestead. Yet I knew the serpent in our northern garden was my lack of time to write creatively in my harried, solid new life.

Behind the perversions
Not lust for pleasure,
But a cry for justice.
"Symmetries and Asymmetries"

As a bookseller I came across "The Platonic Blow," in eight photocopied pages, copyrighted by the Fuck You Press in 1965, its title page sporting a statement by Kenneth Rexroth ("in conversation"): "Wystan told me that he learned more about writing poetry from writing 'The Platonic Blow' than from anything he had ever written."

I knew from Wystan's private conversation since his Ann Arbor days and from his explicit verses, such as "Aubade" in "Three Posthumous Poems," that he found "The Platonic Blow" too hot to include in his published work. While the substance of this underground pornographic classic is central to Wystan's animal nature and private personality, its explicit lines broke the barriers of permissiveness, causing him to re-press it as a low classic; and by "low" I mean that the poem restricts itself to a lower and a lesser audience than that earned by his broader mainstream poems. Yet, because it is written in lean, pure verse that rings with narrative skill, "The Platonic Blow" is likely to live long in underground literature.

The poem describes the narrator meeting a young man of twenty-four, a mechanic (a "common" hero) standing alone in summer sunlight, a sexual hero-object who willingly goes to the narrator's apartment, where sexual play is immediate and described in clinical detail. Being less than love, or other than love, the sexual play focuses on physical satisfaction, and the word "Platonic" sardonically emphasizes the act.

"The Platonic Blow" is supreme male erotic art, aloof from guilt, oblivious to any social implication; it is not an Adam and Eve situation before the serpent intervenes but an Adam and Adam scene with no possibility of a serpent, the instinctual act of two consenting adults in recreational en-counter. Such recreational joy is accepted in many open soci-eties around the world; but some religiously zealous and militarily manipulated societies often attempt to repress overt sexuality and homosexuality as threats to their control over individuals. As far as ethics and religion are concerned, every student of world culture knows that various Eastern religions, as well as many branches of the Christian religion, accept the ancient reality of homosexual love, on the grounds that a just deity can't condemn animal pleasures and playful aberrations of consenting adults.

Because Wystan composed "The Platonic Blow" in hours of extreme sexual loneliness, it reflects only a troubled part of his whole being—as the Song of Solomon is a spicy slice of the Bible, "The Platonic Blow" is an inflated sexual interlude in Wystan's dynamically varied work. If one accepts Picasso as a master artist, one must accept Auden as a master poet, the Picasso of poetry. Art lovers admire Picasso's Minotaur drawings, but fewer poetry lovers are apt to admire "The Platonic Blow" because poetry is more penetrating, more spiritual, more likely to state or sing items of human awareness that cannot be rendered in other media. Even so, Auden's pornographic classic is a devastating tribute to varied human sexuality.

"The Platonic Blow" will prevail as Wystan's "cry for justice," for sexual freedom and social justice, while our open society continues its clamorous claim for all the animal pleasures, all the instinctual freedoms.

TEN

*I, too, would have plumbed
to know you:
I could have learned so much.*
"Posthumous Letter to Gilbert White"

IN THE LATE FORTIES, THOREAU'S EXAMPLE INSPIRED MY "FUNC-tional poverty" life-style, and though I mentioned Thoreau a few times to Wystan, he hardly responded. When Wystan's warm essay on Loren Eiseley appeared in the *New Yorker* in 1970, I studied it and found that Wystan made no mention of Thoreau's influence on Eiseley, so I went to see Wystan in New York and told him that he *had* to read Thoreau.

"And just why do I *have* to read Thoreau?"

"Because we know that Eiseley read Thoreau and was much influenced . . ."

"Really, now!" Wystan fumbled for a light, intrigued.

"You'll find Thoreau as interesting as Eiseley found him," I was urging, even while I was shocked that such an Oxford don as Wystan Auden knew so little Thoreau.

"I've read *Walden* and 'Civil Disobedience,' yes, and *John Brown*. I've *tried* to read the poems. Isn't that par for the course?"

"Of course not! You must read the *Journal*, one of America's greatest books. Everything Thoreau published was based on the *Journal*. And you know that some academics consider Thoreau to be a cold fish, a pondside character who loved plants and birds more than human beings. Not so! The *Journal* documents Thoreau's concern for humanity, for man's relationship to earth, then to society. He understood the regional Indians better than most of his contemporaries. Finally, there's much between the lines of the *Journal* about the love of man for mankind."

Wystan heard me out, concluding, "Well, if you insist, I'll look at the *Journal*. But the set is out of print, isn't it?"

"No. They're very much in print. Fourteen volumes bound as two, with many of Thoreau's sketches, doodles, line drawings . . ."

"F-fourteen volumes!" Wystan was whispering to himself, shuddering. "Hmmm, how will I ever . . . hmmm. Well, all right—send them to me. But not here—send them to Kirchstetten, where I'll have time to read them."

Wystan was properly excited, now, murmuring, "Of course, I've *heard* about the *Journal*, but I didn't think I *had* to read it." And I advised, "One doesn't have to read all the volumes. Browse them. Wander through them. I know you'll like them."

So I sent them, and Wystan replied:

Kirchstetten
June 1, 1970

Dear Charlie:

Yes, the Thoreau Journals arrived safely, though, for some mysterious reason known only to the Post Office, the second volume came two weeks after the first. I am absolutely *enchanted* with them, and most grateful to you for letting me know of their existence. Wish I could report as favorably on our garden as you can on yours. The Spring here has been unspeakable, and everything is behind and sorry for itself.

all the best
Wystan

The next time I saw Wystan on a trip to New York he said, "You know I did get the Thoreau *Journal*? And I'm grateful to you for putting me on to them. They're first rate, and I thoroughly enjoy them." He said this with all of his latter-day mellowness, in humble tones, so that I had to duck my head, nodding casually to conceal my embarrassment at the oversell, for the *Journal* was from the core of my World Eye Bookshop.

Wystan was intrigued with our Bookshop, and asked, "Just what do people buy from bookstores these days?"

"Besides Thoreau, they buy and read something of everything," I assured him. "People read good books if good books are offered. Ours is a general bookstore, with all categories. We were advised not to stock poetry, but we stock it—we have one of the largest selections of poetry of any personal bookstore. And we sell it. We also sell motor manuals, much 'whole earth' material, and most any publication that we like. And we do have a loyal following."

Wystan wanted to hear about the founding of our Bookshop in 1969 in a county seat that had never supported a bookstore devoted to new and eclectic titles with a world view. Although the town, Greenfield, was itself conservative, it was only a short drive from the throbbing Five College area, which gave us most of our trade. I described to Wystan how we'd found our modest location, painted and repaired the interior, built bookshelves from native pine lumber (whose parent trees we could see from our store windows), how we put in our small-business "eight-day" work week, and how we pampered our clients with personal attention to their reading needs. Our Bookshop became an informal center for intellectuals, artists, bohemians, students, and knowledgeable drifters (of which New England has as many as the West Coast); we hung paintings of aspiring local artists on our walls, hosted poetry readings and promoted the books of area writers. We served a thousand cups of tea to supplement our clients' thirst for good books. Over the years we shared the suffering of our friends' personal tragedies, suicides, elopements, and failures; we survived a series of burglaries, break-ins, robberies, and petty rip-offs, and finally a block fire which destroyed our underinsured Bookshop and the other businesses under its nineteenth-century roof. We relocated, reopened, and continued growing, to the satisfaction of our cross-section of area intellectuals, artists, craftsmen (now craftspersons!), housewives, teachers, children—all who loved good books and browsing or buying them in a warmly personal bookstore. As I told Wystan, "Small is beautiful in the book biz if the bookseller can cope with all the 'human types.' "

Wystan "hmmm-ed" appreciatively and ordered a new book, *Migraine* by Oliver Sacks.

By 1970 Wystan was very much a poet establishment with global support, but in my periodic visits to 77 Saint Mark's Place I saw how little his life-style and habits had changed over the years. His flat still smelled the same, and though his cats were long gone, their ghosts lingered in odorous unswept corners; the clutter was still cozily anarchic, and the same nicked coffee cups waited on the coffee table with creamy dregs drenched in old memories. When I brought Wystan a few bottles of my natural Normandy-type apple wine, just as I'd done in previous years, he was visibly touched. Now the persistent tenement tang of the dusty rooms was sweetened under Wystan's perennial bouquets of words, for he loved to talk, and he loved to listen. His best hours were talk hours, face to face with a friend at home or in a friend's home. He told me of his great talks with Louise Bogan and took occasion to remind me that our admired Louise had once given me first prize in a Hopwood poetry contest, implying that I'd "given up poetry" (which wasn't true, for I was still engaged to poetry if not married to it).

At home on Saint Mark's Place I never heard Wystan discuss the Vietnam War, which he dismissed as "unspeakable —like the politicians that engineered it." At times he had muttered a mild curse against "America's global hegemony," but he was now warily apolitical, even mouthing to me that cringing cliché of the political commentators, "Ya-as, things are bad, and they'll soon be worse." Wystan was home from the wars, seeking peace in words and memories.

After dropping a damning quip about the world's worsening outlook, Wystan would switch to "more profitable topics," as he said, usually daily occurrences, and old friends; but once he veered without warning onto the recent reports of massive radioactive contamination. He spoke sardonically of radioactive clouds "drifting from nuclear-generating nations to descend onto innocent nations." I interrupted, "Yes! It's the work of the Devil!" Wystan raised his head, startled, and grunted in agreement, pleased to hear about his old friend the Devil, who was less dead in literature than God, his interesting opposite.

In later years, when Wystan curtailed his tours, he still consented to appear where a friend promoted or arranged his lecture-reading. At the University of Nebraska, Angelyn Stevens's brother, Professor Oets Bousma, promoted such a lecture, and it went well. Then, a short time before Wystan's departure from America, he agreed with the Stevenses' friends to appear at Olivet College in Michigan, where he had taught in the Writer's Conference in the summer of 1941. Professor Edward Speare later told me a bit about Wystan's Olivet lecture:

> In the discussion period I spoke up: "Mr. Auden, you have written so many poems, plays, essays, librettos and reviews—you have traveled so much and met great and wonderful people, you have been honored—what do you plan now? What do you look forward to now?" Mr. Auden stood there, his head slightly bowed, frowning in concentration, then raised his head, threw back his shoulders and quivered a bit as if standing to attention, and called out, dramatically, "To death!"

This reminded me to respect elders' awareness of the imminent end.

In 1970 and 1971 I was making frequent trips from Massachusetts to Manhattan to finalize the documentary film *Tepoztlan*, which I had scripted, directed, and helped to film in Mexico; and to Wystan over evening drinks I described the mentality of the Madison Avenue producers who were as far removed from the Mexican campesinos' world as the earthy campesinos were from Manhattan. I detailed to Wystan the editing, cutting, and "image" battles I weathered, and how I won my share of them.

"Believe it or not," he said, "I got involved in the making of a documentary film, for a Texas celebration." He mentioned it just as if he'd forgotten his stint with GPO documentary films in England in the thirties.

In all these late talks, Wystan never spoke of his family, though in former years he had mentioned with some pride his brother John, and his nieces. When he mentioned Chester, it was wistfully. "Well, Chester's in Athens, now," or, "Chester's new book of poems will be published soon." Once he mentioned seeing Mary Stevens, daughter of Angelyn Stevens, at Cambridge University in England, where she was writing, among other things, an essay on Wystan's poetry. His old friends were precious to him, and he grieved over the departed.

"You knew Dave Protetch?" he asked, looking at me.

Indeed I did. I had met David at Kallman's Kaverns in Ann Arbor in 1942 when he was a student, and Wystan had met him there on a visit from Swarthmore. Years later Dave became an educated Manhattan M.D. who read widely, loved opera, ballet, and art, and generally proved himself a master of cosmopolitan repartee at Wystan's parties. Dave was dark-haired and plump with a rosy complexion, a merry face, ever warm with animal joy. It was a treat to hear Dave's easy laughter, as I did a few times when I made house calls with him around the Village.

Wystan regarded Dave as a personal friend who also happened to be the physician on whom he depended over the years; he was devoted to Dave as he was to any person who entered his personal life and understood his secrets. Dave was the "Doctor Proper" of Wystan's verses:

> . . . a doctor, partridge plump,
> Short in the leg and broad in the rump,
> An endomorph with gentle hands,

Who'll never make absurd demands
That I abandon all my vices,
Nor pull a long face in a crisis,
But with a twinkle in his eye
Will tell me that I have to die.
                    ("Shorts")

But Dave died first, as Wystan told me, his mouth drawn down as he turned to stare smokily into space, his silence eloquent with his loss. Despite his need for medical advice and attention, Wystan couldn't bring himself to rely on any other general practitioner after David's death.

Few of us realized how much Wystan needed his friends. In the past he had often spoken delightedly of his peers, "Tom" Eliot, Forster, MacNiece, Day-Lewis, Stravinsky, the Niebuhrs, Louise Bogan, and others, some of them swept away by time's untiring broom, the others out of sight or far from his Village retreat. At best, he saw his peers too seldom, and now he saw us few survivors when we chanced to visit his flat, where he was pensively at home to those who had claim on his person or his poetry.

Wystan's loneliness wasn't confined to America, as Albert Stevens told me:

Angelyn and I were in Europe and when we got to Vienna we thought we'd just drop in on Wystan. We drove out to Kirchstetten, and I parked our car by the corner *bierstube* to walk along the lane to Wystan's garden gate. He was sitting at a garden table, his fingers keeping a place in a book while he gazed at a rather clouded sky, thinking. He didn't see me standing there, he was looking at something or somebody far off, perhaps in another world. I dreaded to spoil his reverie, but in a few moments I began to feel that I was spying, so I coughed and rattled the gate until he heard me and slowly got up to come and welcome me. We escorted Angelyn from the car and had an exciting visit. Next day, we came back for dinner, which Chester prepared, and we stayed overnight. Wystan and Chester were very proud of his "complete kitchen," as Wystan called it, showing it to Angelyn.

This was the last time we saw Wystan.

*Farewell, and do not wince at
our sick world.*
　　"Lines to Dr. Walter Birk"

On January 10, 1972, just thirty-two years after my first meeting with Wystan, it happened that I phoned him from Crosby Street in Manhattan after ten P.M.

"Ya-as?" he answered peevishly, after the first ring.

"Hello, Wystan! Charlie here . . ."

"Now, Charlie! Whatever induces you to phone at this hour? You know you mustn't!"

"Oh, sorry. I'm excited. We're on our way to England. Lynn and my son Lark are here with me. . . ."

"Aa-all right, then. Come for coffee at eleven tomorrow, but don't phone me at such an hour as this," and he was hanging up while talking, but I could hear Chester's voice above bed-creaking sounds.

Next morning it was windy, with cold rain but no snow in the air or on the pavement. A friend drove the three of us to 77 Saint Mark's Place, and we arrived just as Wystan appeared on the outside landing, easing his carpet-slippered feet down the wet stone steps. He looked over our heads. He was wearing a dark blue "common" raincoat and clutching a brown paper shopping bag with raffia fiber handles, the empty bag kiting in the rainy wind. His striated face was working above his morning pains, and as he stepped onto the puddled sidewalk he seemed to see us as through a haze, nodding at Lynn and flicking a "pet" glance at Lark the toddler, then saying to me matter-of-factly, "What are you doing here at this hour?"

"Well, last night on the phone you told us to come for coffee at eleven, so . . ."

He replied, brightly: "Oh, I did? Hmmm, then it's, uh, all right." He squinted seriously at me. "I must shop for a few things, but I'll take you up. Chester is there." And despite my murmurs of "We could swing by later," we all plodded up the wet steps, Lynn silent, Lark insisting on crawling up on all fours until Lynn scooped him up into her arms. Wystan puffed ahead of us to push open the unlocked door, revealing Chester sitting on the sofa facing us, plump-pink-nude except for a skimpy blue kimono (reminiscent of the blue-flowered one Wystan sported in early Ann Arbor days). Chester, with an audible intake of air, tried to flip the nominal kimono across his rotund belly while Wystan seemed not to notice his embarrassment, conveying the idea with a shrug, as if to say, "My mate slops around all morning, half-naked." Chester, the golden boy of the forties, was now a balding, scar-faced, and toad-plump man.

Wystan was saying affably, "Chester, here's Charlie with his family. Uh, you won't mind, I'll be back in a jiffy." And away he went, while Chester gave me a blue-eyed sardonic glance as he hopped into the glass-doored bedroom (the former "sun room"), reappearing almost instantly, buttoning into flannel pajama pants. Lynn stared in wonder at the jumbled rooms, Lark toddled about in his sixteen-month curiosity, rounding the low coffee table to examine the heaped ash platter, the likes of which he'd never seen in our "no-smoking" farmhouse. Conning the sad Vesuvius of ashes and smelly cigarette butts, Lark seized a shiny defunct enameled lighter and bit it, testing.

Chester, at ease in a replay of his younger affable self, eyed Lark with mild interest while he asked me about our farm and Bookshop as he lit another "first" cigarette of the day, a feat that fascinated Lark. My son, in his pale blue coveralls, with his plump pink "nursing pad" cheeks and Perry-blue eyes, with his long honey-colored curls, was a baby-sized Dylan Thomas, as Chester noted. Beaming under our gaze, Lark seized an emptied cigarette package, bit it approvingly, and handed it to Chester, who refused it: "No thanks, I never eat those at this time of day. You may have it all to yourself." Lark looked intently at Chester and decided that he was all right, while I watched, pleased with Chester's baby-side manners.

Chester talked about the "strenuous move" from Saint Mark's Place to Oxford and Kirchstetten; but except for a few packing cases waiting to be filled, the rooms were much the same as usual. Lynn ignored our male group and read the shelves, the backs of jumbled books, as if she were in a bookstore.

Wystan soon returned with a few items knobbing the damp paper shopping bag and mumbled approvingly at us as he hobbled into the kitchen. In a minute he came out, squinting at Lark, as if seeing him for the first time: "Uh, a little boy, or a, uh, girl?"

Lynn replied, "A boy!" and Wystan said heartily: "Good!" As if I hadn't written him and talked to him about our Lark!

Lynn looked at me proudly and at Lark exploring on his own while I wondered how Wystan would react to a baby girl: into the closet?

Wystan studied Lark and mumbled, "Uh, I must get something for him." He went to the kitchen and returned with a cracked iced-tea glass filled to the brim with lemon-colored canned orange juice, setting it on the very edge of the cluttered cocktail table, commanding, "Here, Lark! Here you are." Lark toddled toward the glass, studied the situation, peering up at the top of the glass just above his head, and touched it curiously before he backed off, looking to me, then to Lynn as he studied the problem of drinking some. Wystan loomed over him, saying grandly, "All right, Lark, you may drink it later, as you please."

Wystan sat contentedly in his chair, looking at his suddenly acquired family while he talked nostalgically: "I'm sure that no one can complain of my leaving America to spend my last days in Oxford, where it all began. Hmmm, I *was* happy there. And Christ Church College is giving me a "grace and favor" cottage, at a ridiculous rent! How much rent did they say, Chester? No matter, a few shillings a week. And there I'll have a maid to fetch my food and to clean. Someone will be near to look in on me. Here I could have a coronary, and no one would know about it for days!" He went on, reciting reasons and facts for his leaving; he talked with relish, obviously pleased with the prospects of Oxford. Chester nodded agreeably, not contradicting Wystan as I thought he might. Wystan's tone was weary but sprightly, a "had enough" tone familiar to New Yorkers: "You know, Charlie, that New York is a dangerous place. Life is difficult, and too complicated, here. Uhm, I do feel that I've earned some right to peace and quiet."

I thought it extraordinary that Wystan went on and on about his retirement. Why couldn't he just say, "I'm sixty-five, and at last I'm retiring"? As for a possible coronary, I didn't believe it because I hadn't heard any mention of heart trouble in the past; but I had heard Wystan say often enough, "I'll live to be eighty-seven," and I wanted to believe it. More than other people—and probably because of my own good health— I had and still have a mental block against illness, or even talking about it. I was more the fool, after hearing Wystan wheezing toward inevitable emphysema, an illness that I understood too late.

Lynn moved around, watchful that Lark didn't break anything or pull anything down onto his head or bite a rare book. Wystan called out to us, "Who will tend your bookshop for you?" Our Gal Friday will, we explained.

"Hmmm, are you flying to Europe?"

"No," I said, "we don't want to fly, we want to go by boat, but it seems there aren't any this month, except to Portugal or Genoa."

"That could be nice, since you'll want to see something of Europe anyway. Hmmm, train travel is slow, but . . ."

"Worse, Wystan. We don't have the money. We were given New York-to-England fares by friends, and we'll be staying with them. It seems that we must fly to London; it's the easiest, most economical way."

"Hmmm, I fly because I have to. In hours, I'm there."

"You're there if the plane gets there!"

Wystan gave me one of those sharp, illuminated glances, wondering at my tiny fear of flying with a "hmmm!"

We talked about our friends in Devon, our hopes of visiting London, Stratford, and Oxford. Wystan chatted on, as if our travels mattered, as if "green and pleasant" England intrigued him as much as it did us. Lark left his tall drink untouched. Our visit seemed a success—nothing was broken, Lark hadn't demanded a breast feeding (a sight that would have been exotic in Wystan's aerie), and Chester hadn't denounced anyone or anything—so we made to leave.

As we moved toward the door, Wystan began a garrulous monologue, mentioning New England towns, including Middlebury and Northhampton, perhaps because he and I had known those places in the past; and then he began to sum up his move to England, saying, in effect, "Well, Oxford is where it all began, and lucky for me that they are preparing a place for me there. Hmmm, everything will be easier for me there."

At the door Wystan and Chester stood smiling while Lynn got Lark organized (he was quite ready to get onto the stairway, a favorite place for testing his climbing ability), and I felt that Wystan was pleased with my family's visit, so I said quietly, "We do hope to get to Oxford. I haven't been there for years."

"We'll be there, later this year," said Wystan heartily. "Uh, perhaps we'll see you there?"

"Yes, do drop by!" said Chester, as if it were just down the street.

With diminishing goodbyes and a final "See you later!" from Wystan, we were out and away.

While Lynn couldn't be central even to our small talk, she had tacitly understood my feelings in the flat and made the visit pleasant. But a door had closed behind me, part of my life closed, though I wasn't to know how final the closing was until eighteen months later. I walked along rainy Saint Mark's Place with my young wife and infant son; I was now the sweet-sullen captive of a close family, very much the husband and father, even while my mind still visited the substance and symbols of Wystan's life at number 77, his longest residence in any land.

Weeks later, Lynn, Lark, and I (after many adventures in Somerset, Cornwall, Stratford, London, and Ireland) were in Oxford in a "b and b" house on Iffley Road near the Melville Hotel. We spent time at Blackwell's buying books for our Bookshop, and time at the homey King's Arms pub, a place that Wystan knew in earlier days. On a rainy April afternoon we visited Christ Church College, where the gate-and-key man kindly told us, "Professor Auden is expected later in the year." We took tea at Saint Aldate's Church Bookshop and Coffee House: "Lynn, this is just the kind of place Wystan likes!" And he had liked it, as we learned later.

On a glorious April Sunday afternoon, with sunlight lancing Blakean splendor through yeoman clouds, a day rampant with stages of blossoming peach and pear, apple and hawthorne, we rented a punt (spunky with wet plank and wilted bracken) to push through flotillas of Oxfordian punters toward the gray-green Isis-Thames. Drifting past Christ Church Meadows, we craned to glimpse Wystan's "grace and favor" cottage; in a flash of gold-on-green sunlight I fancied Wystan ambling along the meadow to enjoy once more the scene of his "youthful ecstacy" in coming months.

Oxford lulled us with its mixture of medieval and academic charms. We climbed to the peak of Glass House, Lark tickled by indoor treetops. Rain enhanced the smell of new grass everywhere, we trudged down rain-washed streets in cool air to devour our "elevenses" and "ploughman's lunch," our Guinness at King's Arms pub; at night we slept under dripping eaves of "Bread and Breakfast House" (as Lynn called it), where I experienced a recurring dream of living in or near Oxford part of each year. In this dream, Wystan and I continued our long talks, and this led to some kind of salvation, or a vague state of grace. On waking, so near to Wystan's final "nest," I thought of his Oxford poem: "Nature invades: old rooks in each college garden / Still talk, like agile babies, the language of feeling."

But in plain language, Wystan had sicked the bee of death into my bonnet ("I could have a coronary"), even if I was too optimistic a beekeeper to feel the sting. So we continued to enjoy Oxford as we'd enjoyed our last visit to 77 Saint Mark's Place, quick with life, oblivious to Blake's gray-bearded scythe man kneeling on his cloud above Wystan's bookcases. We trekked over Oxford colleges like children playing hide-and-seek in cemeteries, alive with unthinking energy, paying homage in our country manner to an absent friend.

Among those who kept in touch with Wystan over the years in America was Strowan Robertson, and when Wystan traveled or toured in Canada, he visited him in Ottawa and Montreal. Strowan wrote to me:

> My last chance to see Wystan was in the spring of 1973, when I flew to Copenhagen and Greenland for the Canadian Film Board. I proposed to Wystan that I stop off in Oxford on my way back. The Film Board owed me for six months' work, and I was confident a cheque would reach me en route, but it didn't. I had to write Wystan, cancelling my visit. I was sick with disappointment at the time; and a few months later I was enraged when it proved to be my last opportunity to see Wystan alive. . . . How disapproving he would have been that behind my failure to arrive was a financial mess!

Robert Hemenway, the handsome student who came to dinner in Ann Arbor and couldn't hold down his food, was now an author, editor, and traveler. Wystan had sublet the Cornelia Street apartment to him, and once sublet him the flat on Saint Mark's Place. Bob was perhaps the last of old Ann Arbor friends to see Wystan alive. He wrote me:

> I went to Kirchstetten weeks before Wystan's death, but he hardly remembered me (I thought); but why should he? I was one hour late for lunch! Disaster. After lunch, Chester said, "I hope you won't be

upset. What you've just eaten were tripe sausages."
They *had* remembered me: I was the fellow who threw
up Charlie Miller's kidneys.

Because I was in England in early 1972 I missed Wystan's
birthday and farewell party at the Coffee House in Manhattan. Then in September 1973, as in a tropical bad dream, I
walked under a Mexican sun to pick up my daily *Excelsior* in
the plaza of my vacation village, and as I sank onto a stone
slab under palm trees I saw Wystan's ghost greet me from the
headlines: AUDEN MUERE EN VIENNA, AUSTRIA.

On "his last evening as himself," Wystan gave a reading
in Vienna, then was driven to his preferred old hotel, from
which he planned to leave next day for London and Oxford,
but during the night he died alone of a coronary. Chester came
to the room at dawn to find Wystan "turning icy blue on a
hotel bed," as he wrote before his own untimely death, a few
months later.

Wystan was buried in the churchyard at Kirchstetten, a
quiet area for his ultimate at-home.

The death of the poet was kept from his poems. . . .
He became his admirers.

One equinoctal afternoon I came alone to 77 Saint Mark's
Place to sit in pale metropolitan sunlight on cold stone steps,
depressed with the awareness that no doorbell could summon
Wystan from his unkempt flat. I felt that I was now something
of a ghost, complaining about cold stone, plate glass, bricks of
dried-blood color, closed doors, and smoggy windows confront-
ing landscapes of concrete structures outlasting wondrous
human flesh.

How far it was to Ann Arbor!—a place receding into
remembered reality: the college town where I waited under a
stone arch for a foreign poet to step out of his pages, the place
where a "common" friendship was born, where history chose
me to befriend one of its bards.

Saint Mark's Place now tried to console me, for it was the

place where our poet practiced his art in his most enduring home, in an Old World neighborhood of open America that accepted a civil neighbor ever "at home" to his muse.

If Wystan, now "comfy" beyond the human hubbub, knew that 77 Saint Mark's Place was vandalized, the green marble fireplace fronts ripped out and sold to shady antique dealers, if he knew that the owners neglected the building and mined it for rental income, letting it sag in Village decay (far from his fond City!), he would shrug. But I hoped he might approve my visit as I arose from the cold stone and walked from the Place, my mind intact and loaded with vibrant memories attuned to his poems, his affirming monuments to man's contest on earth.

Afterword
and Acknowledgment

IN 1941 WHEN I WENT TO LIVE WITH WYSTAN AUDEN IN ANN Arbor he asked to read parts of my journal, so I gave him some thirties' journals. After browsing them he advised me not to indulge them: "Your journal may slough off your creative urge to write the poem that waits within you. This, uhm, loose journalizing may smother the spark that could ignite something more universal and powerful than your personal, uh, daily cry. You *have* written some interesting passages, such as family farm events, uhm, and dreams, but such indulgence may be smothering your poems. Nor should you be writing novels."

Of course I wasn't able to take Wystan's advice as I scribbled onward in compulsive amateur expression, clasping my journal as "my best friend" (too often my only friend) and my autobiographical farm novel as my true mission. Captive to my conversant mode, I traced Wystan through chronic entries that made this memoir possible.

Shortly after Wystan's death (for which I was stupidly unprepared), I began to browse my old journals in order to relive some of our vanished moments. I was amazed at what I found and often dismayed at what I omitted among a million words; but the clues were constructive. After months of periodic browsing and excising passages, I began to reconstruct our American friendship, a mnemonic adventure happily short of total recall, the journals often standing as (mere) signposts in memory's tangled landscape.

It was characteristic of Wystan to warn me against a journal and not tell me that he kept one in his youth; for vestiges of his journal appear in "Journal of an Airman," in "Letter to a Wound," and in many intimate poems. Toward the end of his life, some of his casual poems, such as "Shorts," "Postscripts," "Symmetries and Asymmetries," retain a journal tempo of self-confession. Thus, Wystan was something of a closet journalizer who employed the journal in effective form, in his poems, and as soon as I realized this, I felt more free to write this memoir.

Yet it was years after Wystan's death before I completed a short essay, "Memories of Auden," which I gave to our mutual friend, Norman Holmes Pearson, who quickly challenged me to expand the essay for publication. This I hesitated to do. After Pearson's untimely death, Edward Mendelson found my essay in the Audeniana left by Pearson, and Mendelson urged me to write more. As the young Wystan might have said, History chose me.

As soon as this memoir was commenced, the Stevens family abetted my project in the wholehearted spirit of their long friendship with Wystan; Angelyn Stevens was eminently helpful. Professors Arno Bader and Warner Rice supplied departmental details; the poets John Malcom Brinnin, Edwin G. Burrows, Richard Eberhart, and Howard Moss offered on-the-spot memories. Strowan Robertson was "a particular source," and so was Robert Hemenway. Robert Giroux offered early authoritative editorial means. Stephen Spender and Richard Wilbur cheered me on at crucial checkpoints; James and Tania Stern offered early Manhattan details; Jacques Barzun became my Gibraltar of counsel; but any errors whatever in any part of this memoir are my responsibility.

John Button, Edward Kallman and Dorothy Farnan Kallman, Lincoln Kirstein, Golo Mann, Ursula Niebuhr, Edward Speare, and Henrietta Zuckerman were supportive and corrective. The Michigan *Daily*, the University of Michigan Graduate Library, the Humanities Research Center at the University of Texas, the John Hay Library at Brown University, and the Beinecke at Yale University gave me access to helpful material.

Throughout my happy task, Edward Mendelson gave strict approval and friendly encouragement. My wife, Lynn, and son, Lark, were faithful believers, as well as steadfast guardians of my study door.

Some of Wystan's friends, now deceased, persevere in my mind as silent partners to phases of this book, especially Chester Kallman, David Protetch, and Jean-Paul Slusser.

I am obliged to Random House, Inc., and to Faber and Faber Publishers for permission to quote from Auden's published poems, and to the Auden Estate, which holds the copyrights.

To Wystan Auden who earned his peace among his poems I acknowledge the glories and responsibilities of a long friendship; and I trust that he would approve publication of these memories as he approved the nature of truth through all his friendships and loves.

Heath, Massachusetts
May 1982

Another Time:
Afterword

A memoir is an informal essay about a person as seen and known by the personal narrator, with the purpose of shedding light and warmth on its subject, thus lengthening its life. Memoirs comply to no formula and no rules, except those of truth and conscience. Brevity is their best guideline.

This memoir is notation, observation and recollection on a long friendship, with no inclination to touch up rough edges and foibles of subject and narrator, who wish to be regarded as individuals, the usual imperfects. Happily, time is not intolerant of growth toward understanding, and true friendship entails growth. Thus, your narrator and subject were perhaps better persons in 1973 than they were in 1940 when this friendship commenced so circumstantially.

'Another time has other lives to live,' Wystan Auden wrote, more than half a century ago. Now in another time this memoir may enable you the reader to visualize the actual Auden who lived and wrote so fully in his American time.

CHM

Index